Azerbaijan

Azerbaijan

Corvina
Kiadó

Mosques · Turrets · Palaces

Photos by
Károly Gink

Text by
Ilona Turánszky

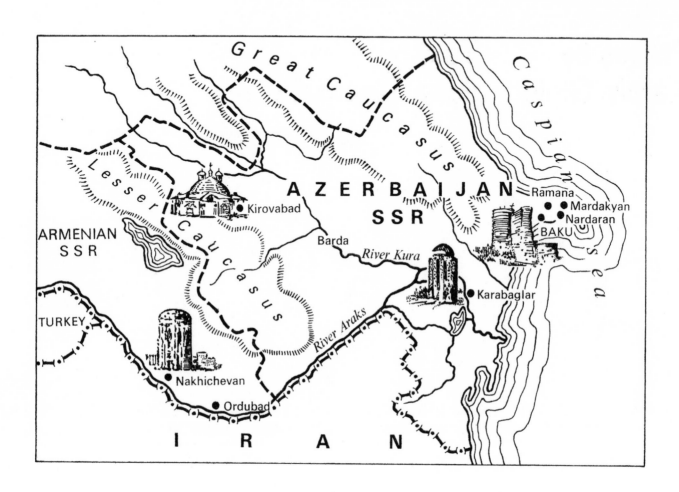

Contents

Original title:
Azerbajdzsán. Corvina, Budapest, 1977
Photographs © by Károly Gink, 1979
Text © by Ilona Turánszky, 1979
First Hungarian
edition © Gink–Turánszky, 1977
Translated by László Boros
Translation revised by Bertha Gaster
Drawings by Zoltán Kemény
Cover, jacket and typography by
István Faragó
ISBN 963 13 0321 7
Printed in Hungary, 1979
Kossuth Printing House, Budapest

Short historical sketch

As one approaches the Transcaucasian states from the north or north-east, the northern slopes of the mountains skirt the Caspian Sea at the city of Derbent. Here, along the main route of the busy caravan roads of old runs the narrow passageway known as the Bab-ul-abvab or the Gate to the East. And indeed, this is where the East begins, the East which differs from the West in its religion and mores, its customs and skills, in its arts, architecture, techniques and attitude to the world as well as in such things as the colour of the skin, the notion of time and the judgement of actions. And, some twenty-five kilometres south of the Gate to the East lies Azerbaijan.

Life at the meeting-point of East and West has always been hard. Azerbaijan has been no exception and its history has consistently reflected the conflicts between the expansionist designs of the great powers of the day. This territory, moreover, has not only been a bone of contention politically, but has also been exposed to cultural conquests from various directions. The roots of Azerbaijani art reach back to influences in the region to the south, primarily to Turkish, Persian and Mesopotamian prototypes, although connections with the art of India and China can also be clearly seen.

For thousands of years this country was an important junction for the trade routes crossing from west, east and south, and the indigenous population were early familiar with a great variety of peoples and customs. Their language is an amalgamation of several ancient and other later tongues. This intermixture is, moreover, not only a characteristic of the language but also of the people of the region. It was therefore quite natural for scholars at the turn of the present century to catalogue the Azerbaijani people as Caucasian Turks or Caucasian Tartars.

For over fifty years Azerbaijan has been a member of the Union of Soviet Socialist Republics. It is one of its southernmost states and the territory — 86,600 square kilometres — is bordered by the Daghestan Autonomous Republic and the Russian Soviet Federated Socialist Republic in the north, Armenia and Georgia in the west, Turkey and Iran in the south and the Caspian Sea in the east. Very few countries in the world can match it for geological variety. In the centre of Azerbaijan stretches the fertile Kura-Araks lowland valley, rich with orchards and tea and cotton plantations. Beyond the river lie the pasture-lands of the Mugan, Mil and Shirvan steppes, their fresh green in spring scorching to a burnt ochre in summer. The steppe is bounded by the Caspian on one side and towering mountains on the other. These are the ranges of the Caucasus which run for 1,100 kilometres, with the highest peaks rising to 4,466 metres in the Great Caucasus and 3,724 metres in the Lesser Caucasus. Above the 3,000-meter line lie the eternal snows unchanging in summer and winter, and under them hidden glaciers have been creeping down towards the valleys for millions of years, inch by inch. The silence is complete; nothing stirs in the wild abysses and depths, bottle-green under their serrated crests. Everywhere below the snow-line, masses of crumbling boulders form impenetrable zones of shale; the steep iron-grey slopes resemble a barren lunar landscape. Below them again rise vertical walls of granite, harbouring here and there the first signs of life: lichen and moss rooted precariously in the crevices. At a height of about 2,000 to 2,300 metres coniferous and deciduous trees have established themselves on the northern face of the mountains, mountains which are awe-inspiring in a raging storm and arrestingly and unforgettably beautiful in the sunlight.

The climate of Azerbaijan is very varied, ranging from the perpetual snow above to subtropical heat below. Storms are frequent, bringing with them waves 11 to 13 metres high in the Caspian Sea; yet in the Kirov Bay to the south the waters are invariably calm. In the nature reserve at Kizilagachi flamingoes, pelicans and swans abound; in the hills to the south and the forests of Talish, tigers and leopards roam.

Some five million people live in Azerbaijan. Two-thirds are Azerbaijanis, a quarter are Russians and Armenians, and the remainder belong to other, smaller nationalities. Half the population is settled in cities; the other half lives in somewhat urban settlements and villages. The principal city of the country is the capital, Baku, with 1.3 million inhabitants. The other cities, Kirovabad, Sumgait or Ali-Bayramli, cannot compete with its attractions.

The Apsheron peninsula jutting into the Caspian Sea, one of the most ancient regions of human settlement, was already inhabited some 30 to 40 thousand years ago. In Kobistan, 60 kilometres south of Baku, traces of prehistoric man have been found. Some two thousand rock drawings that have come to light in the Bayukdash and Kichikdash mountains bear witness to former settlement in this area. These drawings, scratched into the rock walls 3 to 4 thousand years ago, represent mostly hunting scenes. Carved into the more sheltered sides of the rocks in Kobistan, or in recesses less exposed to the elements, are representations of human and animal figures — hunters, dancers, men wearing "tropical helmets", deer and goats — as well as of the big drum, which was beaten as an accompaniment to ritual dances and whose sound travelled great distances.

Archaeologists have made remarkable finds in and around Dassalakhli, a village 10 kilometres from Kazak. More than a hundred caves in the Abeydag mountains revealed traces of Palaeolithic man hidden behind the screen of the natural rock walls, as well as a fair number of tools and pottery shards.

The Neolithic layer produced proof of the domestication of animals, mainly in terms of cattle grazing, and the production of food, and in the Kilik-Dag mountains a flint quarry dating from prehistoric times was uncovered.

Of particular importance are the finds hailing from the district of Khaular, in the area bordered

Nakhichevan. Mu'mine Khatun Mausoleum. 1186

by the Kanjachay and Kurakchay rivers, and in the neighbourhood of the Kilik-Dag mountains where burials dating from the Neolithic and the Bronze Ages as well as attractive pottery—vessels decorated with birds' heads and wings, and lamps in the shape of vases—were found.

The volcanic tufa at Kultepe, some 8 kilometres from Nakhichevan, has long been a quarry for tufa. The hill has been practically demolished when finally the ruins of a small settlement of houses built of stone and mud bricks was exposed. The ruins were primarily of dwelling houses, stables and buildings serving religious purposes. Beneath the debris a considerable number of household utensils and fragments of tools were found in three superimposed layers, the lowest dating from the Copper Age, the middle from the Bronze Age and the topmost from the Early Iron Age. The countless artifacts of daily use, such as arrowheads, jewellery, buckles and art objects brought to light have provided fresh confirmation of the already established fact that iron smelting was known and practised in this region as early as the third millennium BC, to be perfected at a later stage. The spread of iron was of immense economic importance, since the introduction of iron tools and implements considerably facilitated agricultural processes. By this period, one should add, agriculture had become the settled way of life of the people inhabiting the flatlands.

Other archaeological discoveries were made in the foothills of the Great Caucasus, in the neighbourhood of Mingechaur on the Kura river. The superimposed layers yielded not only utensils, tools, weapons, jewellery and vessels dating from all periods between the Early Iron Age (third millennium BC) and the Middle Ages, but also the remains of houses and groups of buildings as well as graves and cemeteries. The buildings included kilns, the foundation walls of temples and private houses; the many graves were varied in kind. One of the most interesting finds came from Zagolu. It was the bronze foot of a throne representing a griffin. Finds closely resembling those at Mingechaur were uncovered in the region of Bayukdash, Yaloilutepe and other villages. Altogether this would indicate that cultural development eventually spread throughout the country.

At the end of the third millennium BC some of the regions of present-day Azerbaijan and Iranian Kurdistan were inhabited by the Lullubians and the Guteans. These most ancient tribes, native to Azerbaijan, were joined during the first millennium BC by the Caspian and Cadusian peoples; later still they were infiltrated by the Scythians and the Cimmerians who came from the north, from the direction of the Great Caucasus. With the passing of time these tribes formed an alliance and established the state of Munna. Their neighbours to the south and south-east were the Medes, whose capital city was Izirtu or Zirta. In the course of its existence the Mannaeans waged protracted wars with Assyria, Urartu and Media. The profusion of archaeological discoveries bear witness to its successive cultures. Eighty-seven kilometres from Evlakh, in the field of Hodjal on the Karkachay river, more than a hundred *kurgans* or *tumuli* were excavated, yielding a comprehensive picture of the succession of cultures in the period between the middle of the second millennium and the beginning of the first millennium BC. A tiny artifact from these graves has aroused enormous interest among scholars. It is a glass bead which, since it bears the name of Adad-Nirari, an Assyrian ruler, can be dated with accuracy: it must have been made at the turn of the ninth and eighth centuries BC.

The simple structures of Cyclopean masonry square or circular in plan, in the area of Nakhichevan and Shamkhora in the southern part of the country, provide information on life in the second and first millennia BC. The huge stone blocks averaging a diameter of three metres weighed several tons each. They were close-fitting, without the use of any kind of binding mortar, the individual blocks having been lifted into position with the help of some unknown lifting apparatus. Most of the buildings were private houses, although among them were quite a few suitable for the storage of goods or stabling of animals, as well as others which apparently served military, defensive or religious purposes.

In addition to providing evidence of a high cultural level in ancient times, the archaeological discoveries made in Azerbaijan also reveal motifs that are still popular in local folk art. This folk art drew primarily on the neighbouring cultures of the Assyrians and Medes, adapting what was taken over to local conditions and individual tastes. The ancient culture of Azerbaijan, concluded Academician N. N. Meshchannikov, was of a peculiar local character which only exceptionally reflected Urartuan influence.

The oldest system of fortifications that has come down to posterity is represented in Azerbaijan by the fortress of Bash-Norasen, dating from early in the second millennium BC. Built on the slopes of the Lesser Caucasus, it consists of two rows of circular ramparts surrounding a citadel and a tower. The defensive walls begin at the bank of the Arpachay river and run upwards to the outer ramparts of the hilltop fortress. Owing to their positions the walls protected not only the fortress itself but also the busy trade route along the river.

The fortress and its defensive walls were constructed of stones placed one above the other without the use of any form of mortar. A highly developed skill in the cutting of stone was essential to hew the huge stone blocks and fit them together to the degree of precision shown here. The only parts of the fortress as a whole to be preserved intact are the black plinths of the carefully polished columns. The masterly way the work was carried out still commands respect today.

The Mannaean state ceased to exist towards the end of the seventh century BC when it was overrun by the Medes who defeated the Assyrians and Scythians around the same time, with the result that extensive regions in the area between Central Asia and the Mediterranean came under their control. From that time chroniclers referred to the kingdom of Mannai, incorporated into the land of the Medes, as Little Media. The domination of the Medes, however, did not endure for long. In 550 BC their country was invaded and conquered by the Persians who also reduced Little Media to the status of a district of the Achaemenids. The Persians in their turn were overthrown by Alexander the Great at the battle of Gaugamela, in 331 BC, when he defeated the Persian hosts and subjugated all the peoples of these regions. Chroniclers report that the Greek armies, and indeed Alexander himself, were amazed by the beauty, pomp, wealth and splendour of the cities they conquered. The great empire of Alexander, however, fell to pieces after the early death of the conqueror. In the territory once known as Little Media, that is, in the southern part of present-day Azerbaijan and in Iran, another independent state arose which was named Median Atropatena or simply Atropatena after the last Persian governor who fell in the battle of Gaugamela. This state, whose capital city was Gazaka, only existed for a hundred and fifty years. Its northern part formed a separate province and was known as Albania. (It is sheer coincidence that this territory was called Albania, since neither the territory nor its people had any connection with the Balkan state of the same name at any period.) This region was populated by Albanians, Legs, Udins and other tribes. The land of Atropatena was very fertile and its agriculture highly developed. "The arable land in the plains of Albania," wrote Strabo, the famous Greek historian, "was better irrigated than in Babylonia or Egypt." It produced an abundance of grapes as well as pomegranates, almonds, nuts and a variety of other fruits. The local population bred cattle and were famous for their iron, bronze, pottery and glass ware.

The land known as Albania, on the other hand, developed more slowly, and an independent state did not come into existence here until the third and second centuries BC, when the region seceded from Atropatena. The ruins of its capital city of Kabala are to be seen in the Kutasheni district.

In 69 BC, after defeating the Armenian king, Tigranes the Great, the Roman general Pompey launched an attack against Albania. The banks of the Kura river were the scene of the bloody battle in which the Albanians were defeated. A tablet with a Latin inscription which had been set up in the mountains of Kobistan recalls the memory of the victorious Roman legions.

The Romans, however, met with such determined resistance that after a while they were forced to withdraw from the territory they had occupied.

By the beginning of our era the peoples of Caucasian Albania had developed a settled way of life. They lived by the cultivation of the land, animal husbandry and their handicrafts, in houses built in organized settlements. The remains of their buildings, engineering works and systems of canalization and water control display a high level of technical knowledge.

Only a few remains survive from the beginning of our era. The most important are the excavations at Kabala. From the first century BC onwards this city is frequently referred to in the writings of Greek, Roman, Armenian, Georgian, Arab and Iranian travellers and historians. It was established along a busy caravan route and grew into a flourishing centre of trade and culture. A network of public utilities covered the territory; drinking water, for instance, was carried by means of burnt pottery pipes to the individual houses. Kabala continued to exist until the fourteenth century AD when it fell victim to the attacks of the Mongols. Today only the remains of the fortified walls, the circular bastions and the huge town gates recall the lost city, together with a certain number of architectural fragments, utensils, tiles, and so forth found on its territory.

The town of Yerendjuk, whose name is found in ninth-century Armenian sources, such as Ioannes Katolikos, and others in the tenth century, such as Stephanos Orbelian, was founded in the first century AD. Written records report that it was situated on an apparently impregnable plateau and the heart of the city, surrounded by walls, was formed by the ruler's palace, the treasury and military installations. Today the remains of the water conduits built of burnt clay, fragments of glazed tiles and a surfaced road bear witness to the existence of Yerendjuk in the past.

The private houses are of particular interest. Those unearthed in the Khanlar district, dating back to the Early Bronze Age, were partially sunk into the ground. Their walls were faced with medium-sized pebbles within and larger stones without. The walls above ground were consequently of two layers cemented together with clay. Buildings exclusively of clay are also known from this period. The roofs of the houses were presumably supported by wooden beams, and the floor was made of *pisé*.

These houses were made up of several rooms divided by log partition walls, plastered over on both sides. The use of pebbles presupposes a high level of technical knowledge since this type of walling demands much greater skill, expertise and precision as well as a feeling for the rules of weight and equilibrium, than is necessary for other building methods.

The simple lines, bright colours and sturdy forms characteristic of the art of nomadic peoples slowly gave way to a highly individual Azerbaijani art which reflected the influence of Persian, Babylonian and Assyrian architecture, modified later on by the impact of the Greek and Roman cultures.

The third century marked another turning-point in the life of Azerbaijan. Early in the century Atropatena came under the sway of Sassanian Persia. Its capital city, Gazaka, became the seat of the Persian governor. Albania, on the other hand, alone among the subjugated Caucasian territories, achieved a certain measure of political independence after peace was signed, following the war with Iran and Byzantium, in 387. In the area under Persian sway Zoroastrianism was proclaimed the state religion. In Albania, on the other hand, Christianity prevailed in the fourth century, Christian teaching reaching the country for the most part from neighbouring Armenia. Together with the Christian faith the Albanians also adopted, without the slightest deviation, their architectural arrangement of the churches and monasteries.

Some of the churches still stand. Twelve kilometres north-west of the village of Kakhi the ruins of a church built on a central plan and dating from the sixth to seventh century, stand desolate in the mountains. At a distance of eight kilometres from the same village, in the centre of Kim on the Kumchay river, the remains of a basilican church with a nave and two aisles dating from the sixth century have come to light. Another sixth-century structure, the church of Kurmuki, as well as the monasteries of Kizilvank and Tsitsernavank are to be found quite intact in the same area.

The church of the Tsitsernavank monastery dating from the ninth century was built of large, carefully carved ashlar stones. Organized as a pseudo-basilican church, its nave is square-ended and at the end of each narrow aisle there is a small square recess, which might have served as treasuries, or perhaps, following the Syrian model, as shrines in honour of martyrs. Both nave and aisles are roofed with barrel vaults. The interior of the church is divided by sturdy pillars, with practically no decoration. The only decorative element on the walls is a ledge of simple design which runs around at the height of the corbels. The structure of these early Azerbaijan, churches faithfully followed the Byzantine models both outside and inside, but they were unable to match the Byzantine artists in the exquisite execution of detail.

One of the most important towns of Albania, Barda, was built at the turn of the fifth and sixth centuries. It is mentioned in quite a few Arab sources which praise its palaces, the mosques built a little later, its caravanserais, covered market-places and many other public buildings. After the demolition of Kabala, Barda for a while acted as the capital city of Albania. Its ruind can be seen today on the banks of the Terterchay river, some 25 kilometres from the railway station of Yevlakh.

In the seventh century another confederation known as Gardman came into being in Albaniai During this period the country, under the rule of the Mikhranid dynasty, lived in peace and prosperity for a period of some fifty years. Close trade relations existed between Albania and

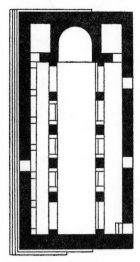

*The church of the Tsitsernavank monastery
9th century. Section and plan*

Atropatena, and a great many irrigation works were established. The oilfields around Baku were already known and exploited and the oil sold. Its jewellery, metalwork and pottery were famous and much sought after, and silk and wool were woven in large quantities.

The towns grew and flourished; several new ones were built such as Paytakaran (today's Baylakan), Khalkhal, Sheki, Shemakha, Shabran and Tabriz, all of which found frequent mention in written records. Some of them, Shemakha and Tabriz, for example, still exist today. Among the numerous remains of buildings of the period the most prestigious are the fortress of Derbent, the so-called "long wall", the castle of Chirakh-kala, the ruins of buildings devoted to religious purposes in the region of Mingechaur, and the bridge spanning the Terterchay at the town of Barda.

During all this period Gardman maintained close cultural ties with Armenia and Georgia. The knowledge and use of Middle Persian, the language of the burgeoning sciences and of literature, spread throughout the country.

This period of peace and prosperity, however, came to an abrupt end in the middle of the seventh century when enemies as yet unknown in those parts made their appearance from the south—the Arabs. In Albania the invaders were met with determined resistance which prevented the consolidation of Arab rule until the beginning of the eighth century. The Arabs spread their faith with fire and sword, levied heavy taxes and the officials of the Caliphate in Baghdad subjected the population to ruthless treatment. The hatred of the people turned against their own feudal lords, who had submitted to the Arabs and entered their service; this led to open revolt which erupted in 816 in the greatest uprising Azerbaijan had known till then.

The leader of the rebel troops was a man by the name of Babek. The hostilities lasted for more than twenty years and in the end the Arabs were driven from most parts of the country. In 837 however the rebels were defeated and Babek was executed. Nonetheless the long-drawn-out struggle eventually weakened the power of the Caliphate to the extent that in the following period several small but independent or semi-independent states arose in the territory of Albania. Of these the state of Shirvan, for a brief period, became of importance. It was in the neighbourhood of its capital, Shemakha, that industry developed in the ninth and tenth centuries. At the same time Barda grew into an important trade centre, referred to as "the Baghdad of the

Caucasus" in written records. And at the same time Baku, Ardebil, Barda and Kabala took final shape.

The country's defence depended on its fortresses and on a network of military installations which, however, was not used in later periods; these were what were called the "long walls" designed to obstruct the advance of potential enemies and at the same time, by their system of fortifications, to safeguard the roads and settlements in the area. The major route linking up the East and West, the caravan road with the heaviest traffic, traversed the country at Bab-ul-abvab, in the neighbourhood of Derbent in Northern Azerbaijan. To defend this route and the northern borders of the country, an extensive defence network had been set up in the course of the fifth to seventh centuries. This was made necessary by the constant wars waged with Iran, Byzantium and the nomadic tribes. The network of fortresses and "long walls" was interspersed with gates which could be closed when necessary; the roads could therefore be sealed completely at Derbent, the Gilgenchay and Samur rivers and at the Bes-Barmak mountain, preventing, for example, the influx of nomads from the north. The fortification system of which the section at Bab-ul-abvab was only a part, protected a very large area.

The walls of Bab-ul-abvab extended over 120 kilometres and were in the main earthen ramparts some ten metres thick. Their southern section was formed by a double row of earthworks running from the flank of the Bes-Barmak mountain to the sea. The fragments of pottery vessels, burnt bricks and utensils found in the vicinity of the walls point to the fact that some sort of settlement had previously existed thereabouts. It is believed that this was no other than the town of Badjarvan, repeatedly mentioned in Arab sources but no longer known today. The section of the wall along the Gilgenchay river was described by Al-Mas'udi, the Arab historian of the tenth century, as a stone wall. Today it gives the impression of an earthen rampart interspersed at distances of some fifty metres by mounds, that is, by the remains of bastions. In spite of all appearances, however, the walls were built of sun-dried bricks and not of *pisé*. The horizontal rows of sun-dried bricks and the fluting two centimetres wide between them are clearly visible even today. The face of the wall was originally plastered with clay, but the top rows of bricks were long ago ravaged by rain and wind and turned into a cohesive mass of clay. The Gilgenchay section of the wall is 30 kilometres long; it is 8 metres wide and 8 metres high. It is estimated that around 50 million large bricks of beaten clay were needed in its construction. These figures give some idea of the enormous effort demanded by the construction of a system of fortification of such proportions.

One of the major strong-points of the walls along the Gilgenchay was the fortress of Chirakh-kala near the main ridge of the Caucasus. A peculiarly shaped rock, as if composed of terraces, served as the natural foundation for this stronghold. To make it more secure the spur of the rock extending towards the mountain ridge was cut, and a deep ditch was thus formed spanned only by the pipes of the water conduit, with a narrow support. The rock offered an excellent vantage-point over the land below. Since it could be well defended from every side, the fortress was regarded as impregnable. Its walls, towers and bastions were built of rough stones with occasional brick fillings set into the masonry. The walls of the fortress keep consisted of alternate rows of stones and bricks.

The storms of the Middle Ages extended to the eleventh century. During that century the Seljuk Turks from Central Asia swooped down, and the weight of their incessant onslaughts brought down these recently established khanates one after the other. It was only the strongest of them all, the khanate of Shirvan, which succeeded in maintaining a certain measure of independence, although heavy levies were extorted for the privilege. The newly occupied territories were settled by Turks. The process was more or less a repetition of what had occurred at the time of the Turkish infiltration early in the seventh century. Although the newcomers were influenced by the local culture, it became increasingly evident that the indigenous population adopted the Turkish religion and customs in every respect, and above all, the Turkish language. The old tribal languages died out, surviving only in traces in the Azerbaijani Turkish which was beginning to emerge at the time. Arabic and Persian, however, continued to be the language of contemporary science and literature for a long time to come.

The admixture of the indigenous population and the Turks was the source of constant conflict. Antipathy and opposition to the Turkish overlords continued to grow. In the twelfth century, during the reign of Manuchekhra II (1120–1149) and Akhsitan I (1149–1203), hostilities flared up anew and with greater intensity than before. An alliance of the original inhabitants with the ruler of Georgia brought its fruits: almost to a man the Turks were driven out of the Caucasus.

The combined victory won over the Turks strengthened the Caucasian states on the one hand and allowed opportunities for peaceful progress on the other. In addition to the traditional crafts of silk weaving and pottery making, the cultivation of the land and animal breeding once again began to flourish. Rice was grown, herds of cattle and flocks of goats grazed on the highland pastures. The fruit grown in the Barda district was famous for its exquisite flavour; the pomegranates and grapes of Baylakan and the figs of Gandja were known and appreciated far and wide. The woollen and silken products of the local craftsmen reached as far afield as Europe, together with fine metalwork and pottery, including beautifully decorated ceramic vases and vessels.

Battle scene. Miniature from the 15th century

Battle scene. Miniature from the 15th century

There was a great upsurge in the arts and sciences all over the East between the ninth and twelfth centuries. Among the many great men of the period were the geographer and astronomer Makki Ahmed-Oglu, from Barda, Bakhmanyan the philosopher, Nizami Gandjevi, and Khatib Tebrizi, a scholar and writer. The royal courts of the khanates, including Shirvan, were centres for groups of scholars, poets and artists, several of whom are known to this day. Independent schools of architecture were established in Nakhichevan, Baku and elsewhere. Much of their work is still in existence, including the fort of Gulistan, the fortresses with their bastions on the Apsheron peninsula, the Maidens' Bastion of Baku, the sunken fortress in the Bay of Baku, the fortress of Alindja-kala, the Mausoleum of Peigambari, the Mohammed Mosque in Baku, the minaret of Shamkhora, the *hanega* or fortified settlement of Pirsagat, and the two mausoleums in Nakhichevan of Mu'mine Khatun and Yusuf ibn Kuseyir respectively. All these buildings display a strong Islamic influence.

Because of its geographical and historical position the influence of two Islamic countries was all-pervading in Albania. One was the empire of the Seljuk Turks, the other that of the Persians. Islamic art first began to make itself felt during the rule of the Arabs (650–837) and achieved its overall ascendancy simultaneously with the beginning of the occupation by the Seljuk Turks (1050). It was only the fortresses and the other military structures that retained their more ancient ground-plans and structural designs right up to the late Middle Ages.

Between the eleventh and fourteenth centuries AD Islamic culture and art drew on a number of sources. Primarily the impetus came from Arabic art, within which wide divergences existed due to local and national features. It also made use of forms of East and South Asian (Buddhist) art as well as Old Persian traditions of patterns. The Turks were a migrant people who at that time had produced no art distinctive to themselves, but they had a flair for adapting and making use of the art of others, and it enabled them to blend the most diverse and often contradictory styles into a single national style. The spatial arrangement of brick buildings around a central core topped by a dome was a specifically Turkish invention introduced in the Seljuk period. For many centuries this was the predominant design for mosques. Two other typical forms of architecture also originate from this period: the minaret and the huge, impressive portal. From this time on the simple gate of two doors of the past was surrounded and embedded in copious decorations of Persian arabesques, floral ornaments and geometric patterns completely covering wall surfaces, together with friezes bearing inscriptions and inlaid patterns, columns topped by capitals imitating those of antiquity, arches and vaults. All these were integrated into an amazing unity of line and colour equal in its intricate beauty to anything Europe had to show.

The predecessor of the minaret was the signal-tower of the Persians. Its major effect was not so much in its power to attract attention, like an exclamation mark, but in the emphasis it gave to the heavy and formal brick blocks with which it was associated, as, for instance, the complex of the khan's palace in Baku.

The minaret formed a single unit with the mosque. There are two types of Persian mosques, the one known as the "arcaded" mosque, and the other a mosque based on a central unit, topped by a dome, with no courtyard adjoining or surrounding it. Traditionally the Persian palace was a domed room on a square ground-plan, with other smaller rooms adjoining one or possibly more sides, and one type of mosque followed this pattern. The entrance to the mosque often faced the large mihrab, that is the prayer niche placed in the direction of Mecca before which the faithful prayed in the open courtyard. The mihrab, moreover, was the most richly embellished section of the building, decorated with painted stucco or colourful tiles, and the mosque as a whole was usually faced with elaborate ceramic tiles.

Another typical Muslim building is the madrassa or religious school. The shape and plan of the madrassa developed in the eleventh century, largely influenced by Persian, Turkish and Arabic styles. This type of building was to spread over Persia, Turkestan, Asia Minor and Egypt. The building enclosed a large courtyard of rectangular shape. Three of the sides held the vaulted cells of the students. Occasionally a minaret was built at the four corners of the structure. The façades were covered with coloured tiles or were perhaps painted, both inside and outside. The more important madrassas also served as mosques, in which case they were usually situated near or around the tomb of some famous sage or saint.

To follow closely the development of the mausoleum or tomb in this region is to become aware of the admixtures of styles and tradition. The sepulchral tower is based on northern—Caucasian—principles of architecture. The primitive stone towers of the nomadic peoples to the north, however, derived their impetus from Persia in the south. The famous Mu'mine Khatun mausoleum of Nakhichevan (1186) with its polygonal tower, brick mosaics, a bright facing of coloured glazed tiles and stucco relief ornaments in the shape of stars and geometrical designs is to be included among the achievements of Persian architecture, even though the sepulchral tower may itself be Azerbaijani work. A special type of sepulchral tower is the domed cylindrical tower, which evolved under Armenian and Hittite influence and spread as far as Eastern Iran. The sepulchral tower fell into disuse, being replaced by the domed sepulchral building which developed from the form of the palace, the timber dome of which was replaced later by a dome built of bricks. The thick walls and vaulting of these buildings were covered with decoration. The amalgamation of the sepulchral tower and the domed sepulchral building produced a type of tomb which was later to spread among the Turkmens in Central Asia, and even later to

Egypt. Here the domed building, so to say, abutted a tower, of massive brick construction some 40 metres high. The sides of these buildings were adorned with reliefs in brick and with inscriptions. They were also frequently used as signal-towers.

The first and principal focus of Islamic display and grandeur, however, has always been the palace, a structure of Persian origin. The façades of these buildings, no matter with how much or how little decoration they were embellished, never began to rival the luxurious magnificence of their interiors. Here we find ourselves in the fabulous world of the Thousand and One Nights. Soft lights, gently splashing fountains, pools set with marble or mosaic, artificially trained or even man-made trees and bushes were to be found everywhere. The walls were almost completely covered with paintings, carpets, mosaic, vases and mirrors. The most important rooms were invariably situated in the middle of the building, on the ground floor with the less important rooms grouped around them or above on the first floor. From the women's quarters the reception rooms downstairs, which these same women could never enter, could be observed through the *shebekes* or decorated lattice-work openings. Trellises on the roofs were covered with plants and foliage, and provided small shady nooks and corners against the heat of the sun. The upper floors were also directly accessible by concealed staircases.

The Persian palace was characterized by an unbelievable display of pomp and magnificence. The throne room of Shah Abbas I, for example, contained 40 columns wonderfully and intricately decorated. The whole of the vaulted ceiling of this palace in Teheran was gilded; its pool was set with silver reliefs glorifying the deeds of the Shah. The rooms were in addition embellished with fine carpets, jasper inlay and precious vases. In Azerbaijan this style of magnificence was exemplified by the palace of the Shahs of Sheki in the Nukha region.

The caravanserai, which was modelled on the private house, was an important institution throughout the Orient in medieval times. They were generally built along the roads, and consequently questions of safety and defence were of considerable importance. One side of the rectangular inner courtyard was taken up by the stables, facing the rooms of the travellers on the other side. The caravanserai was generally a two-storey building if it stood on some busy route. The stables would then be situated on the ground floor and the sleeping chambers on the upper floor. Access to the building on all four sides was by well-protected gates.

Bridges were another notable feature of Islamic architecture. They were arched structures, usually on two levels, built of stone or brick.

Through the intermediary of the Seljuk Turks and the Persians, Islamic art spread throughout Azerbaijan as elsewhere, retaining most of its characteristic features. Local or national differences found expression in the dimension, colouring and decoration largely surviving from old traditional styles. This architecture of the tenth to fourteenth centuries, of Turkish-Persian origin, but remodelled in Azerbaijani fashion, was marked by restraint, simplicity, lucid arrangement and the use of logical forms, heavy and massive in its structure and with a minimum of decoration. Although these somewhat austere principles of building were to a large extent modified in the centuries to come, Azerbaijani architecture never reached that stage of decoration which was so characteristic of Persian art.

From the twelfth to the fourteenth century the decorative motifs most frequently employed were geometrical; they were used on buildings as well as in mosaics, wall paintings and reliefs; they edged the doors and windows, the vaults, gates and tombstones in endless borders. A simple or complex mesh of squares, triangles, circles, polygons and stars was found eminently suitable to cover large surfaces and these motifs are frequently found forming bands or rosettes. The rosettes in turn were capable of endless variation, and when placed in a line close to one other, formed in themselves a ribbon ornament. They were also used to break the monotony of a large surface or to give special emphasis to some point in the design.

The economic and cultural upsurge of the twelfth century was followed by unexampled disaster — the ravages and destruction caused by the Mongol hordes. On a day some twenty years before the armies of Batu Khan sacked Moscow and Kiev and then devastated Hungary, after a broad sweep around the Caspian Sea from the east, they appeared in the Caucasus. In AD 1221 and 1222 they made repeated onslaughts on the region, looting and laying waste. Flourishing towns were razed to the ground, arable land and orchards reduced to barren fields, the networks of irrigation canals wrecked and left to disintegrate. This tragic period of Mongol-Tartar rule did not end before the close of the fourteenth century.

By AD 1400, however, the Mongol Empire was falling to pieces. The occupied lands were freed one after the other, as in the Khanate of Shirvan and neighbouring territories, where the states of Ak-Koyonlu and Kara-Koyonlu came into being. It took only a relatively short time for the Azerbaijanis to rebuild their towns and villages and about the same time they proceeded to strengthen their political ties with Russia where they sent envoys and extended their trade with the merchants of Tver.

Despite the depredations of the Mongols a whole series of architectural monuments have come down to us from the thirteenth and fourteenth centuries. These include the palace of the Shirvanshahs in Baku as well as the fortresses of Mardakyan, Nardaran and Ramana. Mausoleums dating from the same period have survived in eleven places. It was also around this time that the Djuma Mosque in Baku and the minaret of Shikhova were built, together with several civic buildings and a large number of irrigation networks.

The second half of the fifteenth century saw the Persian Safavid dynasty setting out to conquer the country. This family, reported by some sources to be of Azerbaijani origin, recruited considerable forces from the nomadic Turkish tribes living in the Caucasus region. The leaders of these Turkish troops were known by the local population as kizil bashis ("red head") from the red ribbon worn on their helmets. In the autumn of 1500, led by Ismail I, the kizil bashis forded the Kura river, occupied Shemakha and Shirvan, went on to rout the forces of Ak-Koyonlu and finally entered Tabriz, where Ismail I proclaimed himself Shah. He thus founded the Safavid state, which was to play such an important role in the history of Azerbaijan.

Since the victory and accession of the Safavid dynasty in 1500 was owing to the aid of the nomadic Turkish tribes, it was only natural for those Turks who had distinguished themselves in the campaign to be given leading positions in all spheres of public life. The bodyguards of the Shah came from the ranks of the kizil bashis, who were also given the posts of military chiefs, court officials and so on. It was from this time that Azerbaijani was adopted as the language of diplomacy, and it was in this language that the poets wrote, the best known of whom were Habibi, Hatai and Fizuli. This period produced the first popular epic, the *Kör Oglu*, or the "Blind Man's Son". The essays of Iskanderbek Munshi, the historian, and the illuminated manuscripts of the miniaturist Kemal-ad-din Behzade of Tabriz were famous. Trade and handicrafts began to flourish once again. A huge building programme was begun, which included military fortifications, new caravanserais and bazaars. The harbours of Baku and Derbent were built around that time, and new extensions added to the palace of the Shirvanshahs in Baku; a summer palace was built for the Khan in Nardaran. Also dating from the period of Safavid rule were the famous Tuba Shah Mosque of Mardakyan and the Blue Mosque of Tabriz, the tomb of Diri Baba in Marazakh, the mausoleums of Der, Ardebil (of Sheia Sefi) and Shikhlyar (of Sheia Yusuf), as well as the caravanserais of Apsheron, Sangachal, Kobistan, Miadjik and Hilmill.

As early as AD 1300 the arabesque based on floral motifs became popular. At first it appeared alongside the geometrical ornamentation of previous times but later it practically replaced it. A loose or closely woven pattern of tendrils, branches, leaves and flowers covered the surfaces, arabesques were frequently employed to form ribbon ornaments or rosettes, and script, usually the Arab, Kufic or Neskhi scripts, was also used as a decorative element. Reliefs were in a variety of materials and shapes, painted, burnt into glaze or woven into carpets. In general, the inscriptions were surrounded by moresques or arabesques or inset in ribbon ornaments, rosettes and so forth, designs occasionally patterned with such complexity and luxuriance that they tended to disappear or to be indecipherable. Inscriptions were very seldom treated in isolation, as it were, set against their architectural background. When they were, the text worthy of such treatment was usually framed and sited in some important place in the building, most frequently over the gate.

The buildings, following the traditions of Islamic architecture, were built of stone in the north of Azerbaijan and of bricks in the south. The stone buildings were decorated with carving; those of brick provided an opportunity for ingenious and gay decoration in the construction of the walls themselves. In addition to courses of bricks projecting from the wall-face, ridges and ledges and the comparatively simple techniques of various rhomboid or square patterns worked out in brick, glazed tiles were also used as wall facings in the south, a practice adopted from the Persians. The use of coloured tiles was introduced in the fourteenth century and continued well into the seventeenth. The facings were characterized by the most delicate and expert combination of colours carefully designed to separate the main from the secondary motifs. True, the architectural effects of light and shade so effectively used in earlier days were lost, yet they were counterbalanced by the brilliancy of the tiles.

The colours of these ceramic tiles primarily depended on the raw materials used in their production. Usually the pigments most resistant to corrosion were favoured, which is why dark and light blue tiles predominate. Other colours in frequent use were red, white and a blackish lilac, yellow and green occurring very infrequently and then only in minute quantities.

The famous tiles of Azerbaijan with their wonderful patterns, each more exquisite than the next, have been a subject of interest to a number of scholars. The *mokhandisi*, the men who made them, were highly skilled. In addition to having all the laws of geometry at their finger tips, they were master draughtsmen and understood both the decorative elements in the art of the Middle East and the motifs stemming from Azerbaijani folk art. Symmetry was a dominant characteristic of both geometrical and floral ornament. This has meant that repeat patterns were used either in their original form or reversed, sometimes filling a whole surface as with wallpaper, sometimes not more than a single band, the endless repetition of two or more intertwined motifs producing a sophisticated pattern.

At the end of the sixteenth century the Safavid state again found itself at war with the Ottoman Turkish Empire. The war, waged for the control of the Caucasian states, put a severe strain on the Safavid state of Iran. Taxes were raised, internal strife broke out, and as a result the authority and power of the kizil bashis were undermined and the key positions in the state slipped into the hands of the Persian lords, who took full advantage of the situation. The capital was soon moved to Isfahan.

The principal buildings going up in the sixteenth and seventeenth centuries were the east gate of the Shirvanshahs' palace in Baku, the mausoleums in Kalakhar, Khudayarl, Yanuh, Susa, Saritan and Arbil, the mosques of Apsheron, the Djuma Mosque in Kirovabad, other mosques in Yanikhil, Buzob, Nardaran, Mardakyan, Kara-Bazar and Ordubad, the sepulchral complex of Ardebil and the tombs of Sheia Djuneid in Hadjal, Sheia Shahabaddin in Akhar, Sheia Djebrail in the neighbourhood of Tabriz and Gey-Imam in Gandja. A great many caravanserais, baths and bridges were built during the same time, the fortified walls of Baku restored as well as a new fortress, the Chingiz-kala fort, built in Djari.

The conflict between Turkey and Iran, fanned by the French and the British, resulted in a tense international situation in the 1620s, which Peter the Great of Russia promptly exploited to the full, in order to win control over the region round the Caspian Sea. He was successful, and extended his frontiers, almost without meeting any resistance, to the borders of Azerbaijan and Daghestan, thus becoming their immediate neighbour. As late as the 1730s, Azerbaijan and Daghestan were still under the rule of Shah Nadir of Persia, so weakened by economic difficulties, lawlessness and internal disorder that the territories situated at a safe distance from the Persian capital could proclaim their independence. By the time the Shah died in 1747 no less than fifteen small khanates had come into existence on the territory of Azerbaijan. Of these the khanates of Sheki, Karabakhch and Kubin were the most important.

Fearful of the Turks and Iranians as potential conquerors, the Khan of Kubin looked for possible allies, and justifiably, as it proved. At the end of the eighteenth century the Shah of Persia, Aga Muhamed, decided to put an end to these small khanates. He set about the task with utter ruthlessness. He launched an attack against the state of Karabag, crushed it, put the capital to fire and sword, and massacred the majority of inhabitants. Even so he failed in his plans, for it was a long time before he was able to regain control of this small country.

It is true that the conflicts of the seventeenth and eighteenth centuries were an obstacle to progress, but this period also produced work in the arts and sciences testifying to the skill and talent of the people, such as the poems of Vagif and Vidad, the accounts by Hadji Zeinal-Abdin, a geographer and ethnographer of Shirvan, of his travels in Central Asia and the Balkans, the mausoleums of Nakhichevan and Shemakha, the mosques of Nukha, Belokanakh, Agdama and Barda, the fire-worshippers' temple in Ateshga, the khans' palaces of Nukha and Sheki, the palaces of Nakhichevan and Susa and the fortresses in Askeran and Susa.

It is clear from this account that the people of Azerbaijan lived in conditions of hardship and danger in the Middle Ages. Their situation resembled that of Armenia and Georgia in more than one respect. All three countries were often threatened by the expansionist policies of great powers and were in fact attacked by Arabs, Persians, Turks and Tartars. The constant wars of defence against foreign invaders and the struggle waged against oppressors are similar in all three cases. A great many religions were forced upon them, including Christianity, the teachings of Zarathustra and Islam; and many diverse customs, standards and forms of art were integrated into their way of life. Yet the historical road they travelled was not identical in all respects. Armenia and Georgia were immediate neighbours first of the Hellenic then of the Roman Empire, and in fact one time or another formed part of the latter. Later they maintained contacts with the Eastern Empire. Although they were influenced by Greek and Roman art, they successfully maintained the use of their own mother tongue and from AD 301 Armenia remained resolutely faithful to Christianity.

Azerbaijan, on the other hand, was remote from Europe and European influences; the peoples with which it maintained close ties were of Baghdad and Persia, the Turks and the Tartars. They used their languages in speech and in writing, adopted the customs and were influenced by the arts prevailing in these regions. There are a number of similarities between the peoples living in the Caucasus but there are at least as many differences. Here, in a high mountainous region Christianity and Islam met, the hat and the fez, the low-cut dress of the West and the veiled face. The European Baroque and the eastern style characterized by the ogee arch lived side by side. They met, but never mingled. For a thousand years they existed side by side, jealously guarding their own characteristics.

Early in the nineteenth century, the Caucasus attracted European attention, and the Russian Czar and the Shah of Persia vied with each other for its possession. Russian troops occupied the fort of Gandja, one of the main strategic points in the region, in 1804, and the following year, the Czar succeeded in signing treaties with several khans which ratified their countries' union with Russia. Two years later Prince Tsitsianov, as the commander of the Russian forces, besieged the city of Baku.

The war between Russia and Persia ended with the signing of the treaties of Gulistan (1813) and Turkmenchay (1828). Under these treaties Northern Azerbaijan passed to Russia and the southern parts of the country remained within the Persian borders. From this date the two halves of Azerbaijan followed separate roads. An economy based on feudal traditions was retained in the south, while in the north an economic and cultural revival began, made possible — to some extent — by Czarist rule, despite its colonizing policy. Reforms were introduced in Northern Azerbaijan, followed by the liberation of the serfs in 1870. Towards the end of the nineteenth century and in 1900, the railways connecting Tbilisi (Tiflis) and Baku, and Baku and Moscow respectively, were completed. Since oil, "the black gold", made the area of Baku of special importance, hosts of entrepreneurs swooped down on the city in the 1860s and 1870s.

The Mausoleum of Sheikh Khorassan on the Alindja river. Late 12th century–early 13th century

Mardakyan. Fortress

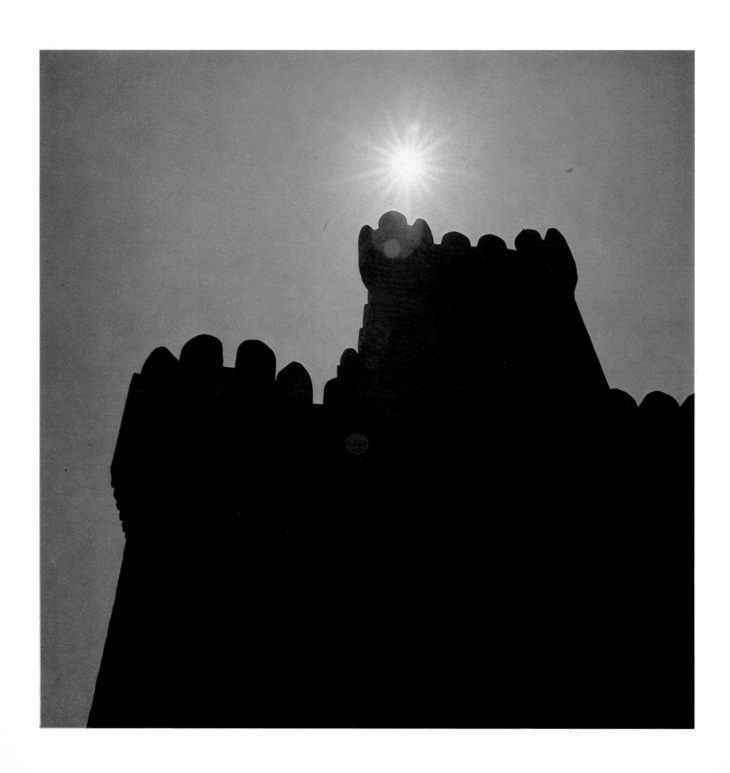

Oil production continued to expand, extensive investments in the oil industry were made and masses of people looking for work swarmed to Baku from all over the country. In addition to Baku other industrial centres with a sizable labour force developed in Kedabek, the home of copper work, and Sheki, the centre of silk weaving.

The first group of Social Democrats was organized in Baku at the end of the 1890s, followed in 1901 by the establishment of the Komitet which professed Leninist ideals. The leaders of this group maintained close connections with the editorial offices of *Iskra* and with Lenin himself. The organization of the general strikes of 1903 and December 1904 as well as those of 1913-14 was associated with the activities of the Komitet.

Six days after the October Revolution, the proletariat of Baku, led by the Bolsheviks, seized power. The bourgeoisie, however, refused to concede defeat and were by no means resigned to the loss of the then highly profitable oil fields. With Turkish and German military help they launched an attack against the Bolsheviks and after a month-long struggle ousted them on August 1, 1918.

The workers, however, refused to surrender. Led by the Bolshevik Party, an uprising took place on April 27, 1920 which ended capitalist and feudal rule. The Revolutionary Council of Soldiers in Azerbaijan was set up and shortly afterwards the Soviet Republic of Azerbaijan was proclaimed. In 1937 the country joined the USSR under the name of the Socialist Soviet Republic of Azerbaijan.

Approaching the country today, either by air, rail or road — the latter running along the routes followed by the caravans of old—coming in from the north, that is through the Bab-ul-abvab, the visitor is greeted by a variety of beautiful landscapes much of it unchanged for thousands of years. The traces of Oriental life or Oriental customs, however, are today few and far between. It is only in small villages that occasionally, and very infrequently, some glimpses of it can be seen in old people's costumes, or caught in a tune, or reflected by an amulet. The new housing estates in the cities are the same one would meet in Paris or Berlin; parts of the landscape have been transformed by the derricks of the oil wells, the huge concrete walls of the power stations, the forests of chimney-stacks and the implements of a mechanized agriculture as in any other industrially advanced country of the world. But here and there the visitor will find some relics of Oriental culture still enduring — the bastions of ruined fortresses, minarets — some jealously guarded architectural remnants, such as the carved tombstones of cemeteries, as well as the faded leaves of manuscripts lovingly preserved in some museum or library.

The Art of Azerbaijan

Baku

Baku lies on the hills surrounding the horseshoe-shaped bay of the Apsheron peninsula which juts out into the Caspian Sea. The great stretches of water, glassy as a mirror, the gently descending crescent of the hills and the town fanning out from the meeting-place of hill and sea present an arresting view.

The heart of Baku is the old town of medieval origin, encircled by a conurbation of streets and squares built at the turn of the present century in the Western style. With their well-arranged and effectively designed components these districts resemble the inner city of Vienna or the districts of Paris bordering the Seine. On the outskirts of this older conurbation still newer housing estates are springing up. These three zones of the medieval town, the conurbation built at the turn of the century and the modern housing estates, all encircling one another in concentric rings, give Baku its particular character.

The three zones remain quite distinct, and their architectural styles never overlap. They form a town structure which is quite unique in the world.

Archaeological discoveries dating back some 35 to 40 thousand years ago reveal that Baku and the surrounding country were already inhabited in prehistoric times. Ptolemy, the Greek geographer of the second century AD, listed no less than thirty settlements in Caucasian Albania by their names. Two of them — Gaytar and Bakura — were pinpointed by him as situated at the mouth of the Kirus river, known as the Kura river today. One of them may well have been the predecessor of present-day Baku. Due to its position Baku has long been a place of strategic importance, enhanced by the fine quality of its soil and a fertile, flourishing agriculture. Priscus Rhetor, the Byzantine emissary to the court of Attila the Hun in the fifth century AD, referred to the permanent fires burning at Baku. By them he certainly meant the natural fountains of inflammable gas from the Caspian Sea.

By the first century AD Baku was already a flourishing town, as shown by the excavations conducted by V. N. Leviatov in 1945. Living quarters dating from the eighth and ninth centuries were discovered in the courtyard of the Shirvanshahs' palace, several metres below the foundations, confirming the continuous habitation of the site.

The present name of the town is first encountered in the work of an anonymous Arab historian and geographer, who described Baku in the tenth century as a small town situated on the shores of the Caspian Sea. The importance of the town was primarily due to the oil extracted in its neighbourhood, although the place was also reputed for its salt-pans and its harbour. Al-Mas'udi, the tenth-century traveller, gave a detailed account of the oil fields to be found in the Baku area. A little while later numerous Arab sources are found recording the exceptional mineral wealth of the town.

In Russian sources dating from the fifteenth to the nineteenth century the town is referred to as Baka, whereas in the accounts of Western European travellers the name is usually written as Baku or, more seldom, as Baki. The name Baku may have originated from the word *bad-kube*, or a place where wind blows, although this could simply be regarded as popular etymology. Another explanation traces the town's name to the Bakan tribe. Place-names adapted from tribal names are certainly of frequent occurrence in this region.

Not much is known of the early town; only infrequent references to it can be found. The most ancient remains are the foundations of the Maidens' Bastion dating from the fifth to sixth century, and the Sinik-kala, a minaret known as the "demolished tower". The latter was built in 1078-79 as part of the Mohammed Mosque.

The Maidens' Bastion and the town wall were originally situated right on the seashore. Later, however, the waters of the Caspian Sea receded, with the result that a fairly wide strip of dry land was created between the walls and the sea. Portions of the ramparts surrounding the medieval town might have existed as early as the eleventh century, even though the first document referring to their existence is of a later date: it is an Arabic inscription recording that the Shirvanshah Abul-Hidja Manuchekhra II (1120–1149) "ordered the rebuilding of the town walls". It was around this time, in the twelfth century, that the seat of the Khanate of Shirvan was moved to Baku from Shemakha.

Practically every architectural style in Azerbaijan's medieval period can be seen in the old walled town of Baku, which stands out like an island amid the surrounding districts. The cul-de-sacs, steep alley-ways, flights of steps and maze of tiny streets as well as the flat-topped buildings with their countless small courtyards, terraces and arbours are precisely the same as they were several hundred years ago. Because of the variety of historical monuments, great care is taken in the preservation of this old district, even though not everything it contains can be regarded as of artistic value in itself.

Baku: the Sinik-kala Minaret

To the left of the narrow passageway leading from the Maidens' Bastion to the fortress stands the oldest Moslem remains of Azerbaijan which have come down to us intact: the Mohammed Mosque and the Sinik-kala Minaret connected with it. A tablet on the wall to the left of the small entrance to the mosque records the date of the building (1078-79, the year of the Hegira according to Moslem chronology) and the name of the architect (Muhamed ibn Abu Bekr). In the world of Islam the arrangement and measurements of mosques and minarets were theoretically defined by strict rules. There were, however, loopholes in these rules which made it possible to deviate slightly from the prescribed canon, primarily regarding the actual execution, materials and ornamentation of the work. Not only were there differences between the mosques built in Turkey, Egypt or Persia, but also on any one single territory; and as a result, several types of mosques and minarets developed in Azerbaijan itself. The differences are mainly to be accounted for by the availability of local building materials and the use of local folk-art motifs. The Sinik-kala Minaret, built in a style typical of the northern region of the country, has preserved its original form down to the smallest detail. The sturdy cylinder built of unplastered bricks tapers towards the sky. A narrow winding staircase leads up to the balcony and is reached from a small entrance gate. The ornamental design of the low stone balcony parapet is of the simplest character. The somewhat crude motifs of the parapet are direct and very simple. Its polygonal ornamentation is made up of six-pointed star formations, a popular pattern in Azerbaijan at the period, and the parapet is supported by a stalactite vaulting running beneath it. Immediately below a quotation from the Koran in archaic Kufic encircles the whole minaret. The Sinik-kala Minaret is far simpler than minarets of a later date. Its large, severe mass, its unplastered walls and restrained decoration bear a resemblance to the towers and bastions of fortresses. The adjoining Mohammed Mosque was built in the same period. Since it was customary to build the new mosques on the site of the old, making use of the remains, it may be assumed that an earlier mosque occupied the same site. The arrangement and structure of the old building was often repeated without the slightest change.

The theory has been advanced that at one time the minaret might have served as an observation tower which, however, lost its role and importance when the Maidens' Bastion was completed at the end of the thirteenth century.

Baku: the Maidens' Bastion

This circular bastion 17 metres in diameter and about 30 metres high is situated at the lowest point of the wall encircling the old town. No manuscript or book on Baku fails to mention it, and there is no painting or drawing of this town on the Caspian Sea which omits it. The bastion is shrouded in century-old legendary tales and mysteries. The stones clustering round the Maidens' Bastion revive old memories of famous historical events such as the story of the Fire Girl who defied the enemy. The hero of the Azerbaijani popular epic, *Kör Oglu*, for instance, also puts in an appearance in these legends. It also presents a number of architectural puzzles, unsolved to this very day.

The name of the bastion is Kizgalasi in Azerbaijani. The word means girls' or maidens' castle. (The strict mores of the Caucasus region took it for granted that girl or maiden should mean one and the same thing.) According to popular belief the bastion was never taken by the enemy. The huge bastion is flanked on the seaward side by a massive wall of almost identical height, as well as by two huge structures, very like bastions themselves. It is not yet clear when and for what reason this enormous bastion system, with measurements quite unusual in both Persian and Turkish architecture, came into existence. It was undoubtedly built for defensive purposes, because the "pillar" or "pier" known as the "breakwater" in popular speech is completely unsuited for such a function. It is moreover completely solid: there are no rooms inside. Nor could it have been designed as a buttress, for the Maidens' Bastion, with its walls five metres thick, is statically well constructed in itself. So failing any other explanation we have to rest content with the fact that the walls served defensive purposes. The solid mass of stone, 2,900 cubic metres in all, was indeed impregnable by any weapon in use at the time. It is clear from the building materials used and its construction that the bastion was not all built at a single time. The foundations on the rock base were apparently laid in the fifth or sixth century, and the higher parts could have been built as late as the twelfth century. The typical fluted ornamentation of these later sections only serve to emphasize the monumental character of the bastion itself.

The small, comparatively insignificant entrance leads to a large shaft rising inside the structure, which is divided by shallow vaultings into eight storeys. Each of these vaults has a railed-in aperture about three metres in diameter in the middle, and through this opening one can look up the whole height of the tower to the open sky above. This aperture, known as the *opeion*, originally served several purposes: it gave more light to the rooms inside and at the same time contributed to quick communication between the various storeys. At the time the structure was built, the construction of the *opeion* constituted a real architectural feat. The picture presented to visitors today is however a reconstructed view of this peculiar piece of medieval architecture, since the vaultings had to be remodelled early in the present century. But as the reconstruction was not entirely successful, it falls considerably below the original with regard to both lighting and spatial effect.

A room with a low ceiling is to be found on every one of the tower's eight storeys. These

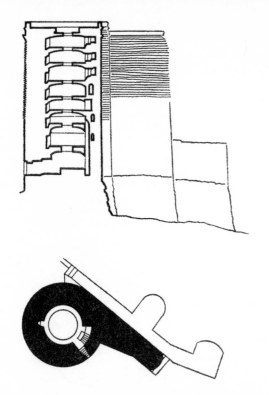

The Maidens' Bastion, Baku.
13th century. Section and plan

various floors are linked by a staircase cut into the wall, with the exception of the ground floor, connected to the first floor by a ladder, which could be pulled up in the event of danger. In addition to the *opeion* the rooms inside the structure received light and air through loopholes or small windows. The tower had a well of its own.

The opening cut in the wall on the fifth floor has been the source of much controversy which will continue, as far one can see, well into the future. Its shape and form shows it almost certainly to have been the opening for a door: the doorsill is level with the floor inside and the places for the hinges and the lock are clearly visible on the doorposts to this day. The walls and the floor of the small corridor which leads to this aperture as well as the doorsill and doorposts themselves show traces of heavy wear; those on the doorsill might have been caused by the tread of human feet, which would be evidence of frequent use. At the foot of this side of the tower are strewn fragments of vaults, pendentives and corbels. They are presumably the remains of the structure which led to the door adjacent the "breakwater".

In the early nineteenth century Russian military engineers made a thorough survey of the whole building and also studied documentary sources and drawings referring to it. They established that the original structure and interior of the Maidens' Bastion was unchanged—at least at that time. It was only the roofs that have been altered and remodelled several times, because they had been adapted as gun emplacements. In the course of time several types of roofs had come into existence, modifying in some slight degree the outward appearance of the bastion and perhaps to some extent the overall skyline of Baku.

Nakhichevan: the Mausoleum of Yusuf ibn Kuseyir

South-west of Baku, in a region of exquisite beauty on the immediate border of Iran lies Nakhichevan, containing two of the most outstanding historical monuments of Azerbaijan: the mausoleums of Yusuf ibn Kuseyir and of Mu'mine Khatun.

The mausoleum of Yusuf ibn Kuseyir, a well-proportioned structure of noble simplicity, was built in 1162 for the great warlord. The octagonal brick building, comparatively small in size,

possesses a tent-shaped roof. The corners of the walls are emphasized by thin pilasters. The walls are faced with an elaborate network of tiles, made up of the most varied geometrical patterns and carried out in earth colours. In the upper part of the mausoleum, which gives the appearance of a tower, and immediately below the cornice runs a frieze with inscriptions in the Kufic script, intermingling with the geometric motifs.

The entrance to the mausoleum is from the west. This section of the wall is the plainest part of the building: it is only the arch above the door and the quadrangular field above that is covered with rows of star-shaped tiles set diagonally. A modest tablet placed in the wall above contains the names of the warlord buried here and that of the builder, Adjemi ibn Abubekr, a master architect of Nakhichevan, together with the date of construction. The arch above the entrance rests on columns whose richly decorated capitals merit the attention they receive from the passer-by.

The interior of the building is divided into two: a high spacious room above and the funerary chamber below. A slope leads to the vaulted lower chamber from the floor of the upper room in the building. The walls have been plastered to smoothness inside and the corners of the octagon, accentuated by thin pilasters, are made of unplastered bricks. Here too a cornice runs round the room where the walls and the vaulting meet.

Nakhichevan: the Mausoleum of Mu'mine Khatun

An especially important place is reserved for Adjemi ibn Abubekr in the history of Azerbaijani architecture. He was born in Nakhichevan, where his three most famous creations are still standing today. They are the mausoleums of Yusuf ibn Kuseyir and of Mu'mine Khatun and the large gateway with two minarets dominating the immediate neighbourhood of the Mu'mine Khatun shrine. His great gifts are best exemplified in the Mu'mine Khatun Mausoleum, which can fairly be described as the most precious and impressive monument of medieval Azerbaijani architecture. It not only gave a new lease of life to old architectural motifs but inspired a new school known as the Nakhichevan school. Architects from this town produced a whole series of impressive examples of Islamic art and were known beyond the borders of their own country, including India. Characteristic of the work was the use of colour—primarily turquoise—in the

The Mu'mine Khatun Mausoleum, Nakhichevan.
1186. Section and plan

tiles which covered both the inside and outside of the building. These enamelled tiles of great brilliance have preserved the radiant lustre of their colours after more than 800 years.

The Mu'mine Khatun Mausoleum was commissioned by Muhamed Djekhan Pahlevi Bey in memory of his first wife 24 years after the mausoleum of Yusuf ibn Kuseyir was built, in 1186. Mention is made of it in a twelfth-century annual together with the madrassa, or school which formed part of it. Although both mausoleums can be included among the tower-shaped funerary memorials, Mu'mine Khatun's shrine outshines its predecessor in size, the richness of its ornamentation and the maturity of its design. The ten-sided building towers over those in the vicinity and dominates the area even today. As drawings, photographs and other sources of the nineteenth century and early twentieth century bear witness, it once formed part of a complex of religious buildings.

A description dating from the middle of the nineteenth century described the course of the building, including that of the mausoleum, in the following words: "The enormous mosque," wrote V. A. Engelgard, "is a conglomeration of vaults which are placed close to or superimposed on one another. In the interior the traces of various types of ornamentation are still discernible, even though a part of the building has already collapsed and the rest is in imminent danger of a similar fate. In the centre the prayer hall is topped by a huge dome, with several small rooms around it. From the outside there is nothing to differentiate it from the usual run of Turkish mosques. Some 50 metres from the building rose the great portal flanked by two minarets, also designed and built by Adjemi. The space between this gateway and the mosque was once filled by an unbroken row of buildings serving various religious purposes."

Mu'mine Khatun's Mausoleum is an imposing brick building. The socle is faced with huge blocks of red diorite, above which rise the walls covered with bright tiles with geometric motifs primarily turquoise in colour. The solid brick structure was originally pierced by openings on only two of its sides; one was the entrance gate and a small-sized window, the other the counterpart of the small window. Each of the ten corners of the decagonal structure are accentuated by projecting clusters of columns; along the top of the wall runs a cornice. The columns and the cornice are enriched with ornate and varied designs and the walls themselves are also embellished with arabesques, interlacing mouldings, drawings and illustrations carved with a special technique. This complex decoration in all its minute and precise detail provides an enchanting contrast to the monumentality of the building as a whole. Above the cornice and the stepped arches at the top of the wall runs a frieze of a brilliant turquoise colour, filled with

Sheki. The palace of the Khans in the Nukha region. 1797. Main façade

Sheki. The palace of the Khans in the Nukha region. 18th century. Painted eaves

Kufic script, intermingled with small reliefs and patterns. Between the frieze and the roof is a line of slightly projecting turquoise stalactite vaulting. The sides of the tent-roof are formed by a smooth surface of turquoise tiles.

The entrance to the mausoleum faces east. The room on the upper floor is accessible through a comparatively small door. The Kufic inscription over the entrance gives the name of the architect and the date of construction.

The two rooms inside, as is customary with the tower mausoleums, are completely independent of each other. The funerary chamber is reached from outside the building. It is a low, rather dark room; the vaulting is supported by a massive pier in the centre. The walls are made up of rows of brick set in an ornamental pattern, which nonetheless in no way relieve the sombre character of the chamber.

The character of the room above is dictated by a quite different set of architectural elements. The vaulted room, circular in plan and 27.5 metres high, gives out a sense of the transience of mortal life, of remembrance and reverence, strengthened by the bare walls—only four rosettes break the plastered surface—and the constant semi-darkness. Originally there were only two small-sized windows; the third was cut in the wall during restorations in the nineteenth century. The gateway with the two minarets, already mentioned, stands in the immediate vicinity of the mausoleum. The design of the gate is identical with those of any other building devoted to religious purposes, or to the madrassa. The vaulted door is framed by bands of ornamentation, and above it is placed a tablet bearing the inscription: "Built by the architect Adjemi ibn Abubekr of Nakhichevan". The highly elaborate ornamentation of the gate is set off by the smooth brick wall where the regular patterns of the bricks are brightened by turquoise pottery tiles.

The Mausoleum of Sheikh Khorassan on the Alindja river

Close by the Alindja river on a bare slope in the mountains of Nakhichevan stands the ruinous mausoleum of Sheikh Khorassan, with three broken columns propped in front. It reflects the particular features of the Nakhichevan school, although the cube-shaped block joining it was only added later, in the fifteenth century.

The mausoleum, built of light ochre-coloured bricks, is a low quadrangular structure, sturdy and large. Above the ground floor it is octagonal in shape, surmounted by a fifteen-sided storey, covered by a dome. The entrance, facing south, is today almost completely hidden

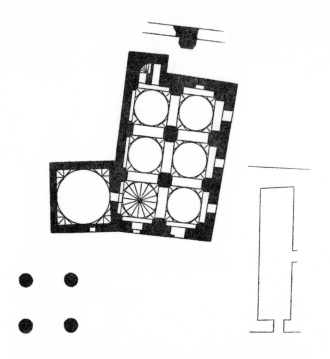

The Sheikh Khorassan Mausoleum on the Alindja river. 12th–13th century. Plan

by the later, fifteenth-century addition. The parts of the gate which are still visible today repeat the style of the Nakhichevan school of architecture. The decoration of the building, especially the use of glazed tiles, reflects the influence of the Mu'mine Khatun shrine.

There are two rooms inside the building in this mausoleum as well. The niche of the mihrab is bordered by an exquisite stone carving arranged in typical fashion. The frame of the mihrab is emphasized by an arch which rests on half-columns. The arch is decorated with arabesques and floral motifs arranged in bands and is framed by plant ornamentation.

The inscription above the entrance and elsewhere lead one to the conclusion that the mausoleum was built either at the end of the twelfth century or early in the thirteenth. One of the inscriptions, in three lines, discloses the name and rank of the Emir who commissioned it and also the name of its architect—Hodja Djamal-al-din.

Baku: the Baylov stones

Not far from the shore in the bay at Baku stands a small island. Baylov island is famous for the stone fragments and the remains of walls found strewn on the ground there. About a hundred years ago, Berezin, the Russian Orientalist, came across the remains of a small fortress which in all probability fell victim to an earthquake. Strongholds of this kind were built at a number of spots in Azerbaijan in the Middle Ages. This fortress had been submerged in the sea for many centuries, but as the sea receded the ruins came to light and explorations were able to proceed. Excavations conducted at the site revealed fallen cornices, vaulting and corbels as well as architectural ornaments and a great number of water-worn stones scattered over a wide area. More recent excavations have exposed a row of pilgrims' cells, with two recesses in each of them.

Most valuable in historical and art terms are the fragments of a frieze several metres long which, it is believed, ran the length of the defensive walls and the turrets. The several hundred stones making up the frieze were reclaimed from the mud deposit of the sea and have been put on view in the inner courtyard of the Shirvanshahs' palace in Baku. The tablets are more or less of the same size: 70–72 cm. high and 25–50 cm. wide. They are adorned with decorative Persian script, various patterns and a number of human and animal figures.

Particularly interesting is the fact that faces with a Mongolian cast of features are to be found amidst the camels and bisons on the frieze. Since the rules of Islam strictly forbid representation of the human figure, which is one of the reasons why painting and sculpture have taken a very secondary place, and pattern and plant designs have predominated in Islamic art, the Baylov stones are of particular interest. The representation of the human figure is very much of a borderline case in the Islamic art of countries such as Azerbaijan. This ban could not be fully enforced in Islamic territories bordering on countries where other religious beliefs prevailed. The decoration on the frieze is extremely varied: abstract motifs alternate with realistic ones, and bas-reliefs so shallow as to appear mere incisions, are found side by side with raised reliefs projecting as if sculpted in the round. Scholars have concluded that the tablets were probably not the product of a single workshop, but were made in different places and in several workshops; it is also possible that the workshops were at a considerable distance from the island, and the tablets were finally fitted together on the spot. The individual details are very varied in style; they are reminiscent of thirteenth-century Georgian, Armenian and Daghestani carvings, but also of the carvings of Vladimir and Suzdal in far-distant Russia, while heads wreathed with diadems and garlands, for instance, clearly show Sassanian influence. The influences shown provide an important basis for reconstructing the contacts Azerbaijan maintained with other countries at the time, and for determining the spread of the different styles and the influence they exercised on one another. What they indicate is that they were known and becoming increasingly familiar.

The inscriptions found on the frieze took considerable time and work to decipher. But from them we have learnt that the fortress was built in 1234–35 by Abu-Rashid ibn Zaid-ad-din of Shirvan. That the craft of carving in stone occupied a position of esteem in its own right is indicated by the fact that the name of one of the master-masons, a man called Rashid, was included in an inscription.

Fortified town on the Pirsagat river

A small fortified town or *hanega* dating from the twelfth to the fourteenth century lies on the road leading from Shemakha to Iran, on the steep bank of the Pirsagat river. It was the most important town in this area, not only at the time it first came into being, but for a good many years to come. As described by one Vassaf, a traveller of the fourteenth century, it was a rich and prosperous place when in 1318 the armies of Uzbeg Khan, the chief of the Golden Horde, passed through the region. According to contemporary sources, the Khan ordered the gold and valuable furs that had been looted from the people of the community to be returned to them. The spacious courtyard of the *hanega* with a bastion at each corner is surrounded by buildings. A minaret, a mosque and several other smaller structures abutted on the defensive limestone walls on the inner side; along the outer side stood the caravanserai and the stables. The most conspicuous of these buildings is the minaret, a typical example of the Shirvan school of architecture. The slender shaft stands on an octagonal plinth which in turn rests on a four-sided socle. The balcony from which the muezzin calls to prayer is supported by a finely carved stone cornice.

The date of building—1256—and the name of the builder—Mahmud ibn Maksud—are known from inscriptions of different periods. At one time the minaret also served as a look-out post. The balanced proportions and exquisite details mark a decided advance on the somewhat primitive and clumsy design of the Sinik-kala Minaret in Baku.

The mosque of the *hanega* was built of finely cut blocks of stone carefully fitted together. The square interior was vaulted with stone, and its floor covered with stone flagging. The finest part of the mosque is the mihrab, sunk into the southern wall, decorated with exquisite carving and flanked on each side with a few small wall paintings. The rectangular frame of the niche and the murals are separated from the bright wall tiles by Kufic inscriptions interwoven with foliage designs.

Adjoining the small dark entrance gate to the mosque rises the vaulted tomb of Pir Hussein. The roughly worked walls and vaulting were at one time covered with splendid ceramic tiles. Especially beautiful is a frieze of some 11 metres long with gold-lustre cobalt and turquoise tiles. The frieze, made up of 600 large Greek crosses interspersed with elaborately patterned eight-pointed stars, runs along the top of the walls, 1.6 metres high, covering in part inscriptions of an earlier date. At one time the vaulting of the tomb was also covered with tiles. The tiles in this tomb are regarded as some of the finest of their kind in the whole of the Middle East. A special characteristic of this *hanega* is that it incorporates decorative motifs from both South

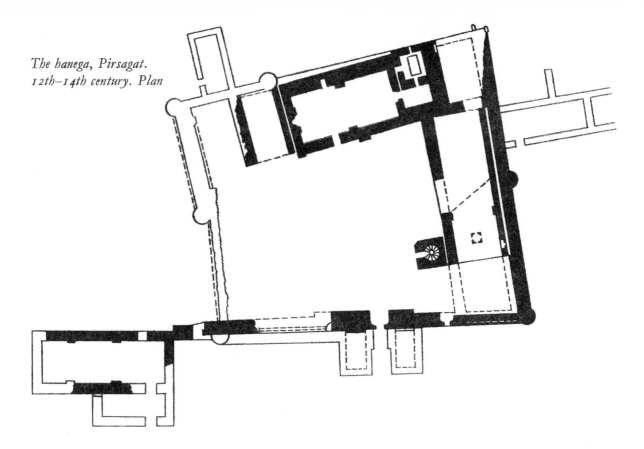

*The hanega, Pirsagat.
12th–14th century. Plan*

and North Azerbaijan; in other words, it is a combination of stone carvings rich in sumptuous details and wonderfully coloured lustre tiles, all the stylistic elements of the period in a new and original fashion.

Medieval bridges

Azerbaijan abounds in rivers and streams, and its roads, both the main highways and those in lesser use, frequently cut across them. As a result many bridges have been built through the centuries, of timber, stone or brick, all of them spanned by arches. The smaller bridges, whose existence is testified by various documents, have mostly perished in the course of time.

But much greater bridges, occasionally of no less than 11 or even 15 spans, were built along the most frequented caravan routes, such as the bridges across the Araxes river and the Hram. Not only were these bridges invariably specimens of first-class engineering, but they were also in themselves works of art, praised by travellers and scholars throughout the centuries.

Of all the bridges perhaps the best known is the Sinik-Körpü or the Red Bridge which spans the Araxes not far from its confluence with the Hram. The ancient road to Iran passed through this spot. The bridge has been generally regarded as a masterpiece of structural engineering. It attracted attention not only by its sheer size, although it is remarkable, the bridge being 175 metres long, but by the engineering skill of its execution. The four spans of the bridge are of different lengths. The piers and the abutments on the river-bank had spacious rooms which used to serve as resting-places. The piers themselves were protected by breakwaters.

The Red Bridge was built in the twelfth century to the designs of Georgian or Azerbaijani master-builders on the site of an earlier structure which had collapsed. According to later Georgian sources it was repaired and restored at various times, the first time around the middle of the thirteenth century. Although the bridge shows a slight Persian influence, certain specific elements in its design place it as a typically Azerbaijani creation. The same is also true of two other bridges over the Araxes at Hudaferin. Although built later than the Red Bridge, these bridges are architecturally somewhat similar. They are bridges of 11 and 15 spans respectively, 100 and 130 metres long and 4.5 metres wide. They were built of roughly hewn stone blocks with a brick facing. Another bridge, at the village of Djuga, also on the Araxes, dates from the twelfth to thirteenth century.

Baku: the ruins of Djebahan Castle

The Sinik-kala Minaret, the Maidens' Bastion and the Baylov stones are by no means all there is to show of medieval Baku. The Tartars destroyed Shemakha, Gandja, Baylakan and a number of other towns, but they spared Baku. Throughout the centuries it is clear from medieval sources that a certain consistency of style and a slow, traditional development characterized the architecture of the town. Such castles, while designed for military purposes, were also inhabited by the people of the district.

There were several castles in Baku although their precise number is not known. One was very recently discovered in the immediate vicinity of the Academy of Sciences. The identification of the ruins was helped by a military map of 1806 giving the name of the building as the Djebahan bastion and arsenal. The fortifications and the buildings inside them date from the fourteenth century, but the arsenal itself is of a later date. The lower sections of the walls and the foundations were exposed during excavations. Considering the intact castles on the Apsheron peninsula it seems safe to suppose that the Djebahan Castle was a huge structure with round bastions at each corner and crenellated battlements projecting from the walls. The ramparts surrounded a comparatively small inner ward with the imposing block of the keep rising in its centre. This was a tower of presumably three or four storeys, with timbered ceilings for the most part, and a few vaulted in stone. A spiral staircase cut into the walls linked the various storeys. Like the four corner bastions, the top storey of the keep was devoted to military purposes.

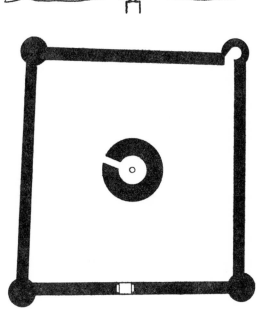

The fortress, Nardaran.
1301. Section and plan

Nardaran: fortress

It is believed that the Djebahan Castle of Baku was a unit in the whole fortification system needed in medieval times, covering the whole country and providing protection against attacks from any direction. The number of fortifications which still survive is exceptionally high on the Apsheron peninsula. Communication between the strongpoints was maintained by fire signals or smoke. A castle in a particularly good state of preservation on the Apsheron peninsula is Nardaran. Two tablets with inscriptions were built in to the carefully plastered wall of the tower; one gave the date of building—AD 1301—and the other the name of the master-mason—Mahmud ibn Saad.

The small castle courtyard is in the shape of a slightly irregular square. The keep of the Nardaran fort is three-storeyed with stone-vaulted ceilings. A spiral staircase leads to the upper storeys. The apertures for light and air are particularly small, even when compared with the small openings of other fortresses. The main defence of the castle was conducted from the top storey of the keep, which is, however, completely in ruins today.

The walls of the fortress enclosure are about five metres thick, the facing is very much rougher than that of the tower, and they have a round bastion at each of their four corners. A walk ran the length of the top of the castle walls with ramparts supported by projecting corbels. The ramparts were pierced with slits at distances of 1.50 metres from one another.

Mardakyan: fortress

Nothing is known about the date of construction and the name of the builder of the fortress at Mardakyan. It was earlier believed to date back to the twelfth century and to have been built by the son of Akhsitan Manuchekhra, the Shirvanshah. It was more probably built in the middle or second half of the fourteenth century. The keep is 22 metres high; a fine view of the sea 2.5 kilometres away and the mainland can be obtained from the top. During the

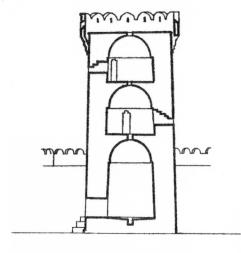

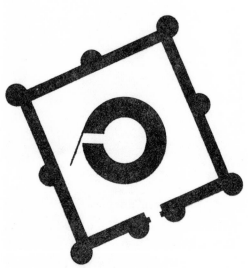

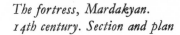

The fortress, Mardakyan.
14th century. Section and plan

excavation of this fortress more than 30 water reservoirs, shaped like great jugs and cut in the limestone rock, and several wells were found within the courtyard, which is 28 by 25 metres. The fortified walls, 6 metres high, also end in round bastions at each corner. The same type of battlement tops the keep and the ramparts. In general the fortress at Mardakyan closely resembles the fortress at Nardaran and the Djebahan Castle in Baku, showing that these strongholds were built to designs which had already matured to an established pattern. But in spite of its many similarities, the fortress at Mardakyan differs in one respect from its counterparts in that its keep is considerably higher. Inside, it is divided into five storeys and the usual spiral staircase begins at a height of two metres above the ground floor. The massive character of the keep is increased by the round bastion at each of the four corners. The finely decorated cornice of the keep is in sharp contrast with the homely appearance of plastered courses of stone blocks and the darkness of the small slits.

Ramana: fortress

Ramana is today a small unimportant village on the Apsheron peninsula. The fortress there, which was built on a foundation of natural rock, is different. The builders gave careful consideration to the configuration of the rock foundation, and as a consequence the walls rise, as it were, as an extension of the rock itself. It is therefore understandable that the castle ward is in the shape of an irregular quadrangle. The gateway opens on to the gentle ascent of the western side and this projecting vaulted structure is a major section of the building complex. Round bastions reinforce the four corners of the castle walls as in the other fortresses, but at Ramana a fifth bastion was also built roughly in the centre of one of the walls, and additional round bastions have been built at the corners of the squat keep. The fortress gate and the entrance

Sheki. The palace of the Khans in the Nukha region. 1797. Interior of the western hall

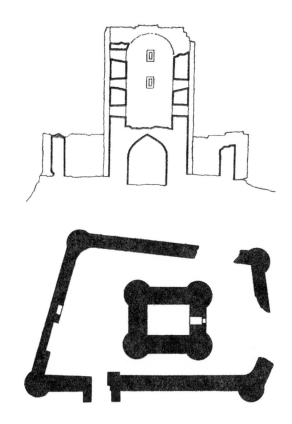

The fortress, Ramana.
14th century. Section and plan

to the keep are arranged so that they cover each other. The spiral staircase inside the tower begins at ground-floor level and connects all four storeys. The lowest and the top rooms are vaulted with stone; the ceilings in between are of timber.

The date of construction and the name of the builder are unknown. Judging from the style and detail, it is generally believed to have been built around 1350, a belief reinforced by the inscription on a stone tablet in the wall above the entrance to the keep which has, however, unfortunately been severely damaged.

Karabaglar: mausoleum

Standing in an empty field on the outskirts of the village of Karabaglar at the foot of Mount Zangezugi are a group of ruins—blocks of stone and the remains of ancient water-pipes—and, conspicuous among them, the great mausoleum of Karabaglar and its two truncated minarets. There are frequent references by seventeenth-century authors to the prosperous town of Karabaglar, lying between Yerevan and Nakhichevan. It still offers a magnificent view against the backdrop of the valley of the Araxes and the plateau of Mount Ararat a little farther off, but at that time it was an important centre with beautiful gardens, some ten thousand buildings, 70 mosques, 40 minarets and a great many other public buildings. All that has survived of this flourishing town is the mausoleum and the two minarets of the huge gate astride the approach road.

The style of the mausoleum is in keeping with the period of Abu Said Bahadur Khan, who reigned between 1319 and 1335. The minarets were built earlier, probably during the twelfth century. Presumably the centre of the group of buildings, devoted to religious purposes, was the mausoleum erected in memory of Jehan Kudi Khatun. The building, formed of twelve intersecting semi-cylinders, rests on a base faced with great stone slabs. The outer wall is decorated with brightly coloured tiles, turquoise predominating. Alternating with the sand-coloured brickwork, the tiles form a simple four-sided network pattern enclosing a milky

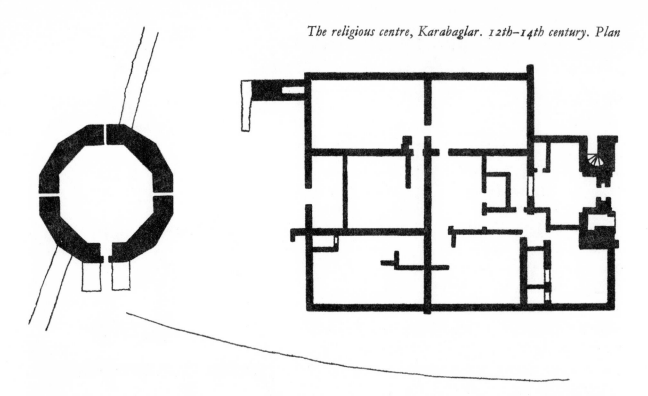

decorative inscription. Above this pattern of the wall runs a wide band of foliage ornamentation on a dark blue ground, and above the frieze the multicoloured tiles of the cornice are, for the most part, no more than fragments, though with a few patches, running consecutively. The roofs and the vaulting, however, have perished completely. The façade is the most beautiful part of the mausoleum but—as was frequently the case in the East in the fourteenth century—it has nothing in common with the interior.

The large room on the ground floor is accessible through four doors arranged symmetrically. Those facing south, east and west are identical. They are formed by columns bonded one-quarter into the wall, supporting stalactite vaulting. The door-case is surrounded by tiles decorated with ribbons of Kufic script. The ornamentation on the western and southern doors is floral, on the eastern door geometrical, and the shafts of the columns are covered with mosaics. The northern door differs from the others in that it is more deeply recessed, the inscriptions are placed differently and the tiles glisten with gold. The very effective difference in the doors may have been a conscious device: it is possible that the builder was inspired by a desire to open up the interior and avoid the traditionally sombre atmosphere of mausoleums.

These four doorways make a Greek cross of the funerary chamber, with a roof of cross-vaulting. The walls are faced with stone slabs. The entrance is from the north. The upper room, two storeys in height, is twelve-sided, with a cornice of plaster and a vault with simple decorations. Near the mausoleum, on either side of the entrance gate, are two truncated minarets. Their bases are covered with a pattern of brickwork. The shaft of the minarets is decorated with a wide band containing an inscription in Arabic. The inscription begins on one of the minarets

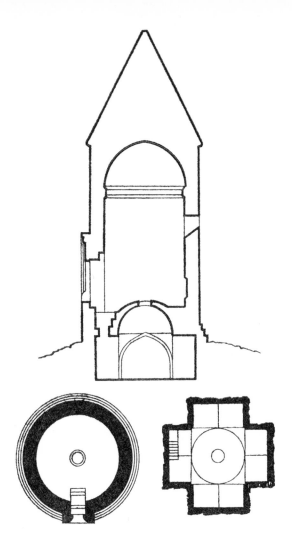

and is completed on the other. The Kufic lettering, in a terracotta colour on a turquoise ground, resembles the decoration of the Mu'mine Khatun Mausoleum. Since the roofs of the minarets have perished, their original form can only be surmised. Inside the minarets there is a spiral staircase of brick, which in the south minaret begins on the ground floor, while in the north it starts from the top level of the building which used to be linked to it.

The building complex of the Karabaglar mausoleum is by no means homogeneous. The masonry of the gate differs from that of the minarets, and its gleaming tiles are less beautiful. The decorative motifs of the mausoleum and those of the minarets are also different. All this tends to show that they were built by several mastermasons with varying abilities and different levels of technical knowledge.

Ashagi-Veysalli: mausoleum

The building known by tradition as the Mir-Ali Mausoleum is situated along the ancient road leading from Baylakan to Barda. Its slender circular shaft is supported by a stepped base and is covered by a tent-shaped roof. It is one of the best examples of the tower mausoleums of the fifteenth century and at the same time one of the outstanding historical monuments of Azerbaijan. Beautiful proportions, architectural regularity, a sober system of decoration and a finely worked stone façade combine into an exceptional whole. Since there is no inscription giving the date of building, it is only from historical sources that one can assume that it was erected early in the thirteenth century. The design of this mausoleum was frequently repeated in later times.

The mausoleum is faced with cut stones fitting precisely; its narrow doorway is framed by a simple border with a braided edge.

The interior follows the same design as that of other funerary memorials: it consists of a funerary crypt and a memorial hall on the ground-floor level. The crypt of the Mir-Ali Mausoleum, however, is accessible by a slope within the building and not from outside as is the case with other buildings of a similar type. The central portion of the crypt is in the shape of a cross, below a shallow dome, and the deep recesses which form the arms of the cross are roofed with barrel vaulting. The floor of the whole room is covered with large, smooth stone slabs.

The hall above is irregular in shape. The arched niche of the slender mihrab is placed under a small window.

Baku in the Middle Ages

Baku was an important city as early as the thirteenth century. One reason was the fact that around that time the main trade routes changed their course: Derbent was eclipsed and it was Baku, where the major routes then converged, that benefited from the change.

The reign of Shirvanshah Ibrahim I (1382–1417) was accompanied by the rapid growth and development of Baku. The Shah was a remarkable politician, skilled in exploiting the conflicts between more powerful nations and thereby safeguarding the peace and tranquillity of his own country. He was, moreover, the first ruler who chose Baku as his capital.

Due to this period of peace, the arts and sciences flourished. As a result, outstanding works of architecture came into being which made the name of their architects known far and wide. Master-builders, for example, were invited to Derbent to rebuild the town, which had been destroyed by an earthquake, and it was then that the columned Djuma Mosque in Derbent was designed by Tadj-ad-Din ibn Musa, a master-mason from Baku. The town walls, castle gates and bastions running around the whole of Baku were built in the fifteenth century. Contemporary sources, such as the records of Sherif-ad-Din Ali Yazdi, the court historian of Tamerlane (Timur Lenk), and of Hondemir, another scholar of the period, give a detailed picture of the fortifications. A deep moat formed the first ring of defence, followed by the outer walls, and inside the perimeter, some 4 to 5 metres apart, by another, inner, wall identical with the former. For ease of defence and attack, the straight line of the two walls was broken at acute angles at several places. The castle gate was even more massive than the walls themselves; they were protected by double security zones. Since at several points the walls projected into the sea they also protected the harbours. There are frequent references in these records to the several underground tunnels that led from the castle and the town to both the sea and the mainland. There were also secret passageways inside the castle buildings and the larger private houses in the town. This skilfully designed and brilliantly executed defensive system served as a model for the planning of other castles by the sea, and also for the reconstruction of the harbour at Derbent.

The most detailed description of Baku in the fifteenth century comes from the historian Abd-ar-Rashid ibn Salih. "The town rises on a rock lapped by the sea. Two of its walls jut out into the sea. They are so massive and strong that they could withstand the onslaught of the Mongols themselves. Without exception the houses are built of stone. The most important mosque in the town is the Djuma Mosque. The air is clean and fine, except for the fierce winds which often blow man or beast into the sea. The soil in the town is infertile and there is only one part of it where gardens of figs and pomegranates and vineyards can be seen. Oil wells also erupt in the town, and oil is not only used locally for heating, but bags are filled with it and it is carried by camels to other countries as well."

As Abd-ar-Rashid ibn Salih remarked, the most important mosque in Baku was the Djuma Mosque. It was repaired and adapted several times from the fifteenth century until the present century, when a wealthy Moslem had it completely restored. The mosque stands in a densely inhabited part of the town, probably on the site of a former mosque. It is irregular in plan—an irregular hexagon with truncated corners to the south and west.

In addition to the Djuma Mosque a whole series of mosques were built in the town during the fifteenth century. These included the Chin, Molla-Ahmed and Hidir mosques. With the exception of the mihrab, the interior of these mosques is generally completely plain, with only a little decoration on the exterior walls, only one or two stone tablets, in addition to the entrance gates, and a few small windows covered with dense lattice work.

Baku: the palace of the Shirvanshahs

This group of buildings, dating from the fifteenth century, is situated on the western outskirts of the Old Town, on the central hill of what is now the modern city of Baku. It is surrounded by a high wall broken by two small and two big gates. This wall interspersed with slits for defence was built as late as the nineteenth century and indeed may not follow the former boundary of the palace complex at all. Old drawings make it clear that the palace was originally surrounded by a warren of alleys and streets.

The palace and the other buildings mount up on three levels. On the highest level stands the shah's palace, the Divan-hane, separated from the central courtyard by another wall, and the mausoleum of the court astronomer Seid Yahiya Bakuvi, with the ruins of a small mosque adjoining it. On the second level stands another courtyard containing the burial place of the shahs and a mosque, complete with minaret. On the third and lowest level were the bath-house and the water reservoir.

Today the palace is accessible through four gates. One of these, a small gate, communicated directly with the Divan-hane, and another opens on to the courtyard in front of the main entrance to the palace. A third gate, which is larger and more ornate, gives access to the second level and the mosque and burial place of the Shirvanshahs. The fourth gate stands at the end of a narrow passage between the palace and the mosque. In the Middle Ages this was a public street. Communication between the courtyards of the palace complex is by way of several passageways and steps.

The palace and the buildings around it were restored in 1920, when later additions were demolished. Today the palace is a protected area. Its museum contains an exhibition of architecture, including historical and architectural relics of Baku and other parts of Azerbaijan, and also the famous Baylov stones.

The floor of the courtyard forming the uppermost level of the whole palace is mainly flagged; the small pools, fountains and flowerbeds which embellish it breathe out the atmosphere of an Eastern fairy-tale. One side of the courtyard is bordered by the south façade of the shah's palace, and the opposite side by the walls of a building erected at a later date, the Divan-hane. From this spot a beautiful view opens out on to the town and the sea.

All the buildings in the palace complex are built of large, grey stone blocks; the smooth surfaces are occasionally broken by exceptionally rich insets of carved stone.

The shah's palace is two-storeyed and was built in the fifteenth century. Its walls are free of all decoration. The entrance gate is exceptionally large, completely dwarfing the small, irregularly set windows. The plans of the ground and upper floors are identical. Both contain twenty-five rooms, most of them small. In the centre of the building is a hall, octagonal in shape, which was originally covered by a dome. This hall formed the core of the building and was built round at later stages. It adjoined an octagonal vestibule reached by the main staircase which was, however, destroyed sometime in the past. In the course of restoration work, in order to protect it from further decay, the whole building was covered by a flat ceiling of iron girders and concrete and the dome was consequently destroyed.

The Divan-hane is in fact a peculiar small courtyard encircled by high walls. Arcades covered with slightly projecting roofs run along the walls; the whole structure resembles the cloisters of a medieval monastery. A domed octagonal building rises in the middle of the small courtyard;

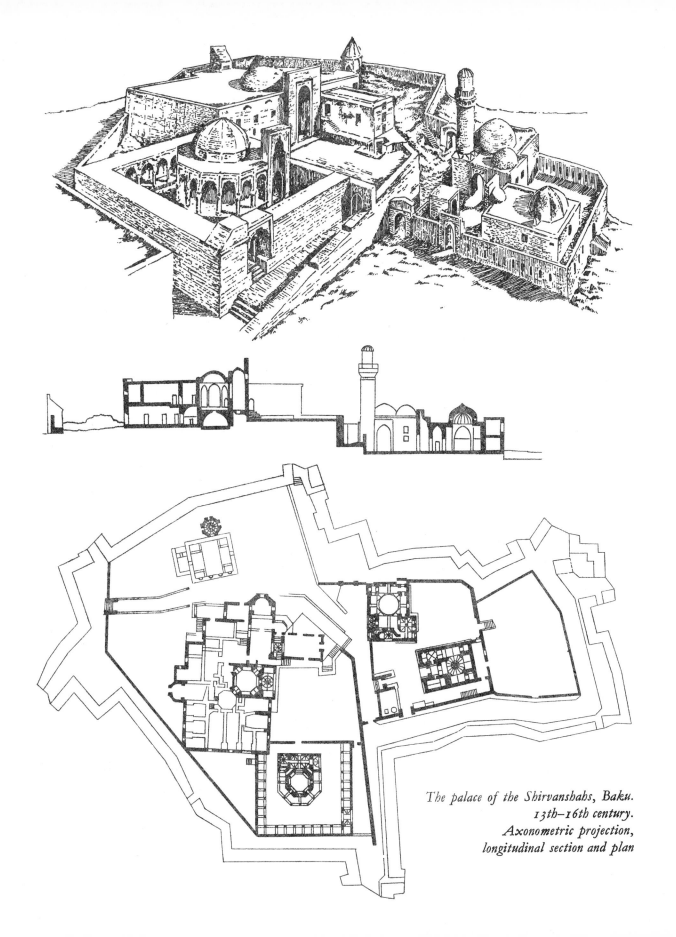

The palace of the Shirvanshahs, Baku.
13th–16th century.
Axonometric projection,
longitudinal section and plan

its main entrance faces west. This entrance with its exquisite carving, beautiful arabesques, the perfect stalactite vaulting of the semi-dome and the profusion of delicate lace scrolling, not to mention the fine proportions, is one of the genuine masterpieces of Azerbaijani stone-carvers. The small building standing in the middle of the courtyard and containing a single room is surrounded by a covered colonnade. It is a piece of considerable architectural virtuosity; the well-proportioned spatial relationships between the parts help to make it the finest section of the Divan-hane as a whole. The columns and their interconnecting arches follow the same design as the arcades running round the courtyard.

The real purpose of the Divan-hane is not yet fully clear. The building is the subject of countless tales and theories. Its name suggests that is was a place where justice was dispensed. The small hall in the centre might have been the court room where the trials were held. Below it there is a small chamber partly below and partly above the ground; it may have been the room where the accused waited to appear. The cellars on one side of the courtyard could have served as cells. The witnesses summoned probably waited in the arcades or the covered colonnade. Others believe that the Divan-hane was a hall for ceremonial purposes, where foreign emissaries were received and councils held. In that case the crypt might have housed the treasury, and the colonnade might have been used by the guards. The latest theory assumes that the building in the centre of the courtyard was a mausoleum and the small room below was the funerary chamber. This seems to be confirmed by the quotation from the Koran in the upper band above the main entrance. "Allah leads all the peoples of the world along the true road. He is good and magnanimous to the true believers. Their eyes will not be blinded by dust, nor can they perish, for they will inhabit paradise for ever."

Many people believe that nothing but the Shah-i-Zinda necropolis in Samarkand equals the Divan-hane. In Samarkand the visitor is held by the magnificence of the wonderful tiles; in Baku he is dazzled by the perfection of the composition as a whole and the flawless and exquisite craftsmanship of the carving. The decoration is inspired by a mind of inexhaustible fantasy and originality, and the building is a monument to the genius of the stone-carvers of Baku and the great fame they achieved.

The date of the Divan-hane has not yet been precisely established. The general assumption is that it was built in the fifteenth century, during the reign of Shirvanshah Farruh-Yessar. It is possible that its construction was interrupted by war, for some of the detail has remained unfinished to this day.

The small courtyard on the middle level contains the mosque and the burial place of the shahs. This small, austere mosque was built early in the fifteenth century. There is no decoration on

Wall ornament. Embroidered cloth decorated with a row of beads and small-sized round metal plates. Gandja. 19th century

Woollen prayer rug. Baku. 18th century

Carpet from the southern Caucasus. Kuba district. 19th century

the exterior of the walls at all; they are perfectly plain, though a few quotations from the Koran have been carved on the wall of the minaret. The gloom of the interior is somewhat counteracted by the well-proportioned dome and the lovely stone lattice work of the windows. The mihrab is separated from the main hall by a low stone balustrade. The slender minaret adjoining the mosque was built in 1441. Both the stalactite corbels which support the stone balustrade and the finely carved inscription running below it are evidence of the high standard of stone-carving achieved in Baku.

The burial place of the shahs closely resembles the mosque in plan, structure and in the simplicity of its execution. This great block of a building in the shape of a prism is dominated by its decorative gate, articulated in much the same manner as the main portal of the Divan-hane. The stalactite vaulting of the semi-dome of the hood arching over the deep recess of the entrance gate is supported by the simple door-case. The walls on either side of the gate are covered by a profusion of flower ornament arranged around an imaginary axis of symmetry. Flowers fill the two decorative spaces, but here carved letters have also been placed by a master's hand. The name of Ali, the founder of the Shia sect, wreathed in garlands, can be seen above the gate. In contrast to the portal of the Divan-hane, the flower ornamentation decorating the funerary memorial *(türbe)* is realistic in design, and as such it is quite unique in Islamic art.

The centre of this building is a domed hall with deep recesses covered over with vaulting on each side and small chambers in the corners. The execution of the interior strictly follows the traditions of medieval Azerbaijani architecture, although, to a certain extent, developing and perfecting them.

In the lower courtyard are the remains of a bath-house and the water cistern, similar to other Moslem establishments of the same kind. The comparatively large entrance led to a vestibule opening on to the dressing-rooms. The way to the pool proper from the dressing-rooms, a central hall covered by a huge dome and with recesses containing smaller pools, was through the rooms for washing.

The cistern was one of the largest in the town. Its vertical shafts allowed air to circulate continuously. The water flowed in through channels from a distant cistern. The engineering skill shown in this installation evoked considerable praise from foreign travellers.

A mausoleum was built in the fifteenth century beside the mosque for Seid Yahiya Bakuvi, a learned court astronomer. The mausoleum, resembling a tower, rested on a simple octagonal base and was covered by a tent-roof. It is generally known as the Dervish Mausoleum. It is a fine building carried out in a simple classical style. Variety is provided by a rhythmical alternation in the size and colour of the stone courses, the careful design of detail, the fine stone lattice-work of the windows and the elegance of the plaited decoration on the interior of the dome. An interesting trick of perspective is provided by the fact that, to enhance the spatial effect, all vertical and horizontal lines are made to converge. The influence of the Dervish Mausoleum in Baku can be seen in several places as, for example, in Shemakha and Hazra.

The most recent part of the palace, the great eastern gate, is in the upper courtyard. An inscription records it as being built in 1585, during the short-lived Turkish occupation of Baku, and also contains the name of the master-builder, Ulu-Radja-baba of Baku. The gate resembles those of the Divan-hane and the *türbe*, but the details differ, primarily no doubt on account of the individual tastes of the builders, but also to some degree because of the different purposes of these gates. The doors to the Divan-hane and the *türbe* were entrances to buildings, whereas the wider eastern gate gave on to a courtyard, and was designed to allow wheeled traffic to pass through. The greater width naturally demanded greater height as well, and in its decoration little delicate motifs were consequently eschewed as unsuitable.

Of the builders and designers of the palace only the names of the master-builders of the eastern gate and the *türbe* are known. Forming part of the decoration of the gate is the name of the master-builder Amirshah of Tabriz. It was most unusual to invite a builder and stone-carver of another town to Baku to be responsible for so important a structure as the eastern gate, but be that as it may, Amirshah of Tabriz produced a fine piece of work. The eastern gate effectively combines forms and types of decoration of both the south and north of the country, again confirming the close artistic connections between the two parts of Azerbaijan. In the Baku palace of the Shirvanshahs, however, can be seen indications of influences from much further afield. There is a considerable resemblance between the marble gate of the Bibi-Hanum Mosque in Samarkand and the gates of the palace in Baku. This is no coincidence, since the famous stone-carver of Azerbaijan, Sherif-ad-Din, worked on the building of the Bibi-Hanum Mosque. This master-builder is reputed to have been born in Shirvan or perhaps in Baku.

The Shirvanshahs' palace in Baku is characterized by the simplicity and austerity of its geometrical forms, and by a logical and rational organization of space. Their combined effect is enhanced by the masterly manner of working the stone. The finely dressed and most varied carvings gave rise to a new style of stone-carving associated with Baku.

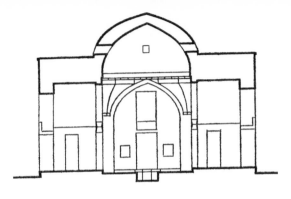

The summer residence of the Shahs, Nardaran.
15th century. Section and plan

Nardaran: the summer residence of the Shahs

The Shirvanshahs' removal to Baku was of great importance in the fifteenth century, not only in the development of the town, but also to the Apsheron peninsula as a whole. The castles gradually lost their importance. In the middle of the fifteenth century, for instance, a mosque, known as the Tuba Shah Mosque, was built in the neighbourhood of the fortress at Mardakyan. At the same time the style of architecture changed.

The summer residence was built in the northern part of Nardaran, about two kilometres from the sea. It is a regular cube in shape, surrounded by a few smaller buildings housing servants, with a pool and two fountains. The side facing the sea is broken by a great gate projecting from the façade and emphasizing the main cornice. Several long windows were placed in the four sides of the palace. The cube-shaped block is crowned by a huge dome over the central hall, resembling in many respects the dome of the mosque in the Baku palace.

The interior is well arranged on a symmetrical design. An interesting feature is the opening of the entrance gate directly into the central hall, and so connecting the interior of the building with the garden. The large vaulted recess in each of the four walls of the domed hall gives it the shape of a Greek cross. At each of the corners is one of the four smaller rooms in the building. The two on the south side are covered by octagonal domes, and those on the north are covered by spherical domes resting on plain cornices.

The satisfying proportions and design of the Shahs' summer residence give it a beauty of its own. The simple style, devoid of any kind of decoration, is more or less along the lines of the Baku palace of the Shirvanshahs. In the relationship, however, between the interior and the natural world of the garden outside it is a late successor of the court buildings favoured by the Sassanid rulers, and this at one time led to the assumption that the summer residence was built in the thirteenth or fourteenth century. It is clear to us today that the historical conditions of the thirteenth and fourteenth centuries made the building of a palace for such a purpose impossible.

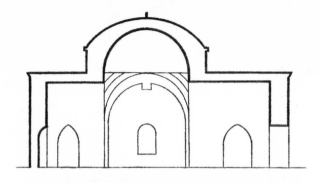

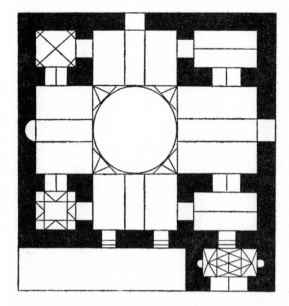

Mardakyan: the Tuba Shah Mosque

In addition to the fortress, the Tuba Shah Mosque is the most famous sight in Mardakyan, attracting attention by its typical form and style. It is an example of the type popular in the north, characterized by a simple plan and a definite spatial arrangement, organically linked with the articulation of the façades.

The beauty of the façade is largely due to the juxtaposition of the plain, carefully dressed grey stone wall and the intricate pattern of the lattice-work in the windows. A simple cornice runs round the top of the walls. The dominant note is provided by the gateway, framed by the traditional ribbon ornament and familiar motifs of the fifteenth-century architectural school of Shirvan, Apsheron and Baku. The stalactite vaulting, the carving of the tympana, the hexagonal rosette above the gate with the name "Ali" repeated six times, are exact copies of the gate of the Baku palace.

The interior of the building is in effect a central prayer chamber in the shape of a Greek cross. The usual pattern is slightly modified by the fact that the entrance to the chamber is on one side, and consequently worshippers entered through a room in one of the corners. The prayer chamber is covered with a hemispherical dome, accentuated by the low drum supporting it, and the *opeion* giving light to the interior. Four recesses, the two on the north side covered by barrel vaults, the two on the south by domes, frame the area beneath the central dome. The dome above one of the corner rooms is exquisitely star-shaped, of a rather complex design. The mihrab is set in the wall which conforms to the south arm of the Greek cross. Its fluted semi-dome is supported by an entablature.

A stone tablet records that the building of the mosque was ordered by Tuba Shah, and was completed in 1483. Another inscription of an earlier date, at the entrance of the spiral staircase leading to the top of the building, informs the visitor that the mosque was built in 1372 by Hodja Hur-ad-din ibn Hadji Bab-Ad-Din and Adayiba ibn Mahmud. The tablet on which

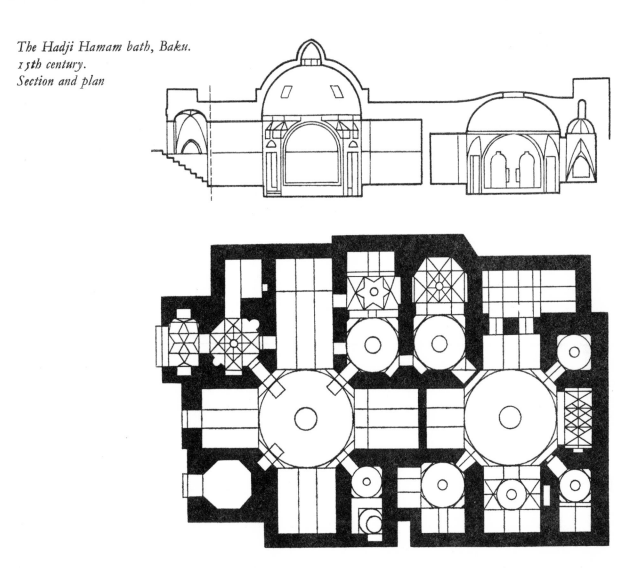

The Hadji Hamam bath, Baku.
15th century.
Section and plan

this inscription is recorded is set in a wall obviously much older than the other. It therefore seems clear that the Tuba Shah Mosque of today was built on the site of an older mosque, or more precisely, around the parts that had survived.

Baths

A good many Turkish baths serving the needs of the Moslems have survived in Azerbaijan. Turkish baths, like the baths of the ancient Romans, were centres of social life and social intercourse. They were designed on mainly functional lines which remained unchanged over long centuries. The focal point of the building was the great pool surrounded by several smaller pools, flanked by rest-rooms and dressing-rooms. The central basin and each of the smaller

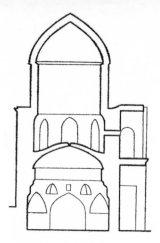
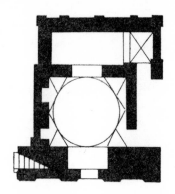
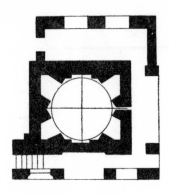

The mausoleum of the religious complex, Kirovabad. 17th century. Section and plan of the two levels

pools were covered by domes. This functional arrangement was completed by an efficient system for the provision of water and heating.

The various Turkish baths still in existence, such as the small Kasimobeka bath of Baku or the Hadji Hamam dating from the fifteenth century, the bath of Nardaran, consisting of a single room, the Sheikh Kasim of Mardakyan, the Hadji Kurban of Lenkoran, the seventeenth-century village baths of Baksal, and a series of other buildings serving the same purpose, are all very similar with greater or smaller local differences expressed mainly in the size and the type of decoration.

Kirovabad: the Imamzade or Gey-Imam Mausoleum

The ancient town of Gandja, which today is no more than a huge mass of ruins, was situated seven kilometres from present-day Kirovabad. The Imamzade or Gey-Imam Mausoleum is located in the northern section of the former town. The name of Imamzade refers to the burial place of a descendant of Ali, since it was only they who bore the title of Imam. When the mausoleum was restored (in 1878–79) an old tablet was affixed to the wall which recorded that the funerary memorial was erected over the grave of the Imam Mohamed Bagira ibn Ibrahim who died in the eighth century. The word "gey" in "Gey-Imam" means blue, and refers to the colour of the dome. The mausoleum was part of a religious centre which ceased to exist long ago. The whole complex was surrounded by a defensive wall with gates. Within it, mosques, funerary memorials and other buildings were grouped around the mausoleum.

The mausoleum itself was repeatedly rebuilt and renewed so that it is difficult to determine the date of its origin and the various renovations. The old tablet cannot be regarded as authentic, particularly as no funerary memorials were being built in the territories of Islam in the eighth century; the earliest originated in the ninth century and were built for statesmen of the highest rank, a category which did not include descendants of the Imams. This is not to say, of course, that the personage buried here could not have lived in the eighth century.

The core of the mausoleum is formed by the part of the tower dating from the fourteenth or fifteenth century; this is confirmed by the photographs taken before restoration work was undertaken. From these pictures it is clear that during the work of renovation the dome and its drum were drastically altered. The photographs show that the original dome was of the type widespread in Central Asia in the fourteenth and fifteenth centuries. The Kufic inscription produced when the individual glazed tiles are correctly combined, is also clear. It is alleged that it was this inscription which was responsible for the reconstruction of the dome. The restoration work was directed by a devout Moslem of the name of Jadigarzade who found the content of the inscription offensive to his own tenets, and consequently had the whole dome demolished and rebuilt.

Undoubtedly, the arcades on two storeys which surround the mausoleum on three sides, as well as the eastern gate, originated in the seventeenth century. This claim is substantiated by the characteristic framing of the arches.

Kirovabad: the Djuma Mosque

The Djuma Mosque of Kirovabad, with a minaret to the right and left, stands in the middle of a courtyard surrounded by a wall. A stone tablet inscribed "Kilidi Shamakha 1606" indicates that the mosque and the other buildings were erected early in the seventeenth century when the inhabitants of Gandja moved to the newly established town.

The builder of the mosque, Sheiy-Baga-Udin, was a well-known master builder of his time. On each of the four sides of the prayer chamber is a recess. The deeply recessed niche of the mihrab is on the south side, and the main entrance opposite it on the north. There is also a smaller entrance on the east and west side respectively. A peculiar feature of the mosque is the exceptional size of the arched openings. The mosque was demolished on the orders of the Khan of Karabah, but was rebuilt again in 1885. It is presumed that the present mihrab with mirrors was made at that time, together with the other ornaments.

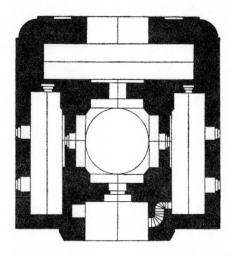

The Imamzade Mosque, Barda. 17th–19th century. Plan

Barda: the Imamzade Mosque

The oldest building in the ancient capital city of Barda is the Imamzade Mosque. It might have been built as a mausoleum originally, and in 1868 a mosque was added to the building. It was a frequent custom of the Moslems to build a mosque beside the funerary memorial of some holy man. Such remodellings or extensions often resulted in the emergence of a completely new architectural ensemble, which was the case here.

The walls of the funerary memorial in question are built of brick and stone, with a minaret rising at each of the four corners of the building. The way the brick courses are set and the ornamental designs are similar to several ancient buildings, such as the Mu'mine Khatun Mosque of Nakhichevan and the mausoleum of Barda built in 1322.

Ordubad: madrassa

This is the only madrassa in the territory of Azerbaijan that has come down to posterity intact. The earliest examples of these religious schools for the training of Moslem preachers date in this region from the twelfth century. These institutions were generally situated beside a mosque and occasionally also served as "Friday mosques". The Djuma Mosques of Kirovabad and Shemakha each had a madrassa attached to them.

The madrassa of Ordubad was one of the major centres of scholarship in the Transcaucasian territories during the seventeenth century. Its plan follows the traditional arrangement of this type of building: the four-sided courtyard was lined by rows of cells one and occasionally two storeys high. The large entrance gate was cut in the main, northern, façade, providing a dramatic contrast to the cell-lined walls. The whole complex is simply carried out with a complete lack of ornamentation.

The cells of the pupils *(hudjra-i tullab)* were small, vaulted rooms; they were windowless and

Woollen prayer rug. Shirvan, Kobistan region. Late 19th century

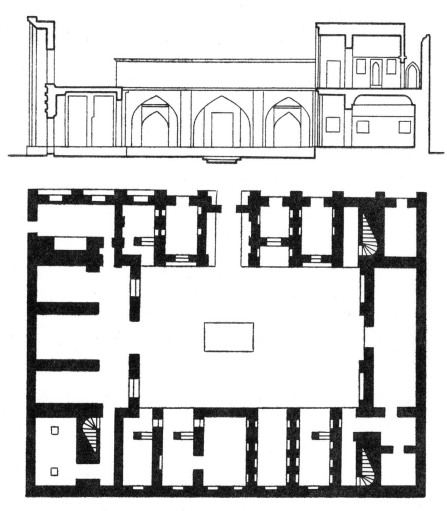

consequently dark, their arched doors opening on the courtyard. On the upper floor there were often no partition walls between two or three cells, an arrangement frequently found in caravanserais. The larger rooms, which served as classrooms, were situated at the far end of the courtyard. A stone tablet in the wall of the madrassa records the date of 1714 when a large-scale reconstruction of the whole group of buildings was undertaken. Presumably there was a building there before that date, built probably in the first half of the seventeenth century.

Baku: caravanserai

In the Old Town of Baku, south-east of the Maidens' Bastion, in the neighbourhood of the Street of the Merchants stands a caravanserai designed with two storeys which is of considerable architectural interest.

Like the madrassa, the caravanserai was a one or two-storeyed building enclosing a four-sided courtyard. This design was well suited to insulate the rooms from any kind of noise or bustle.

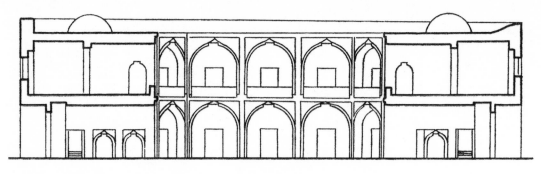

The caravanserai, Baku. 17th century. Longitudinal section

In the single courtyard, however, there was considerable traffic: access to the buildings was chrough or across this courtyard. The windowless cells on the ground floor opened on to this tourtyard.

In contrast to many others, the caravanserai of Baku offered greater peace and tranquillity to its guests. Its buildings surrounded an almost square courtyard 24×27 metres in size. There was an entrance on two of the sides of the courtyard. The rooms were located on two levels, but those on the ground floor did not open directly on to the courtyard, but on to a small anteroom built precisely to insulate the room from the courtyard, with a wall and a door that

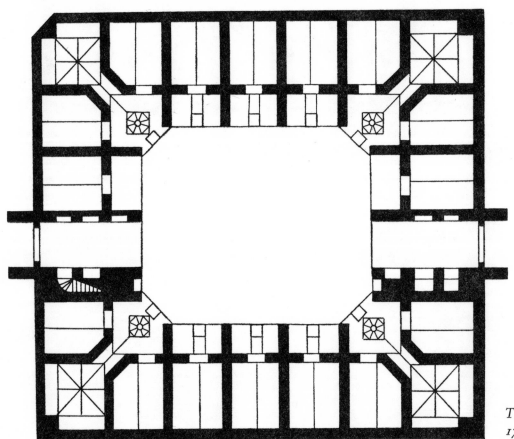

*The caravanserai, Baku.
17th century. Plan*

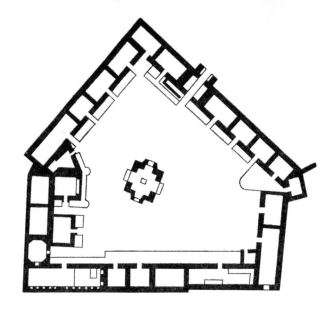

The Temple of the Fire Worshippers, Apsheron peninsula. 18th century. Plan

could be closed. On the upper floor there was a corridor which ran the length of the building between the inner courtyard and the rooms, which unusually had outer windows opening on the street below. The arches of the arcades surrounding the courtyard and the balustrades gave the caravanserai an atmosphere all of its own.

The caravanserai in Baku possessed a further peculiarity, namely, the design and arrangement of its four corner rooms, providing a double anteroom before these corner rooms. One of them was a large, square room opening on to three other rooms, and another, a small anteroom like a corridor, opening only on to the corner room itself. This arrangement gave the four corner rooms a more isolated position and less noise than the others, and in addition their windows opened on to the street in two directions. Two staircases with small recesses beneath them connected the two floors of the caravanserai.

The Temple of the Fire Worshippers at Ateshga (Apsheron peninsula)

The Fire Worshippers' Temple at Ateshga was given its contemporary appearance in the eighteenth century, yet it mirrors the ancient architectural tradition of the locality down to its smallest detail.

Twenty Sanskrit inscriptions were placed in the temple in the course of the eighteenth and nineteenth centuries. The earliest written sources refer to Ateshga as a Persian shrine of the Fire Worshippers or "Hebro". Shortly afterwards comes the first mention of fire worshippers from India. The Sanskrit stone tablets are irrefutable evidences of the Indian connection.

It is possible that this building was the temple of Indians who settled here at the beginning of the eighteenth century, but the possibility cannot be ruled out that the temple has a history reaching back to earlier times. The building surrounds a pentagonal courtyard which is surrounded by a wall of medium height. The battlemented walls are irregularly interspersed with slits. The windowless cells of the pilgrims back on to these walls. The cells are of varying sizes; they are completely plain and their only furnishing is a cot recessed into the rear wall. Beside the gate stands a small tower with a room a little larger and better lit than the cells on the second floor, presumably designed for the accommodation of more important visitors.

The shrine is in the middle of the courtyard; it is in fact a square pavilion topped by a small onion-shaped dome. Chimneys were built at the four corners of the open pavilion to which natural gas was channelled in pipes and then lit. A fire also constantly burnt in the heart of the shrine. This was the holy fire, the object of worship for the pilgrims.

Sheki: the palace of the Khans

Within the fortified walls of Sheki, inside the fort, stands the palace of the Khans of Sheki. Most of the buildings forming the complex and dating from different periods have been destroyed; only the palace or summer residence has come down intact.

The palace was built in 1797 during the reign of Muhamed Hassan Khan. The arrangement of the two-storeyed building is the same on both floors: three large rooms separated by two anterooms. But they served entirely different purposes, and there was in fact no immediate link between the two. The ground floor contained the offices, accessible to the clerks working there and the petitioners, no matter how humble. The upper floor, however, was reserved for the privileged, for the guests of the Khan and their relatives; it was the women's quarters.

The main façade of the palace looks south, toward the town. It mirrors the inner arrangement of the building, the three large rooms and the two anterooms within are reflected in the wall sections with rows of windows and deeply set arched recesses. The small coloured glass panes, geometric in form, are fitted into an intricate pattern of lattice work. The window-bars are painted decoratively. The windows and walls provide an elaborate ornamented setting for the arched niche of the entrance and the galleries above.

The wall paintings in the interior of the building deserve special mention. All the rooms, down to their smallest corners, are without exception bright with paintings, carvings and inlaid decorations. The wall paintings date from different periods. Those of the greatest value, of the eighteenth century, are in the main halls on the ground and upper floor. They are patterns of geometric and floral design, scenes with figures in them, and bird and flower motifs. The wall paintings cover every possible part of the walls: the spaces between the windows and above the doors, and so on. The subject is frequently dictated by the shape and size of each wall section; the narrower and longer areas filled with plants springing from a vase together with flowers and scrolls, somewhat wider bands being decorated with birds on a branch and encircled

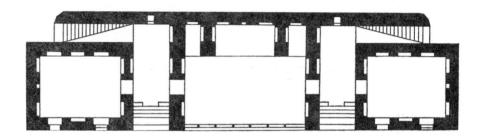

*Sheki.
The palace of the Khans,
Nukha region.
18th century. Plan*

with flowers. On the wall between the first and second niche in the large room on the upper floor, a frieze depicting a hunting scene can be seen. The most vivid of the pictures are those painted with tempera on a plaster ground.

Five artists have left their signatures in the midst of these decorations. The earliest is that of the master-builder Abas-Kuli who, interesting enough, has recorded his name twice, on the ceiling of the large upper room, in a sequence from right to left, and then in reverse. He was possibly the builder of the palace as well as one responsible for some of the decorations. A number of the paintings in the ground-floor rooms were by Mirza-Djafar of Shemakha, painted in 1895 and 1896. Usta Gambar of Susa painted some of the works in the upper-floor rooms. His signature and the date (1902) was found in the upper part of one of the niches. Rooms of the upper floor were decorated by Ali Kuli and Kurban Ali of Shemakha.

The palace of the Khans was built in a period when architecture in Azerbaijan was on the decline. Even so the standards are high, reflecting the strength and inexhaustible wealth of traditional folk art.

Ordubad: private houses

A great many distinctive types of private houses developed in Azerbaijan over the years. Urban houses differed from village houses, and those in the plains differed from those in hilly regions. In general their foundations were of stone, on which were superimposed walls 60 to 80 cm. wide of beaten adobe bricks. Burnt bricks, however, were used for vaulting or small domes. In the towns two-storey dwellings were frequent. Their fronts were occasionally narrow, not more than four to five metres, but the buildings reached far back. The closed privacy of the façade is a distinctive feature; practically no openings give on to the street, with the exception of a few very small windows arranged haphazardly and the entrance gate, designed to give emphasis to the building as a whole.

Inside, facing the courtyard, the aspect is completely different. Here a friendly, almost romantic atmosphere meets the visitor, who finds himself surrounded by exquisite carving, painted door-panels, vaults, niches, loggias, terraces, door-hinges, knockers, handles of wrought iron—even the top of the nails were decorated. Many of the walls were covered with paintings, and oriental carpets were strewn about the rooms. Flowers, fountains, pools and arbours were to be found

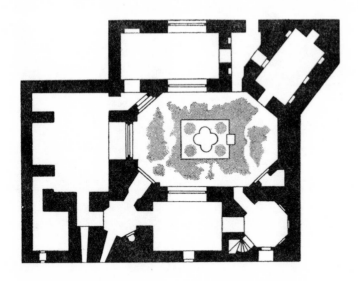

Ordubad. Private houses. 19th century. Plan

under the shady trees of the courtyard; a most pleasant micro-climate to give relief even in the hottest seasons. The centre of the house was invariably a great polygonal room, giving on to almost all the rooms in the house. It also opened directly on to the garden and provided access by a staircase to the upper floor. The ground floor of the two-storey buildings was generally devoted to offices and the entertainment and accommodation of male guests; the women's quarters were on the upper floor.

Private houses in the country were more spacious. Typical of them was an underground area covered by a dome which more often than not also covered a well. This room was the storehouse for food, and naturally was the coolest of the rooms in summer. The ground on which the building stood was invariably surrounded by a high and solid adobe wall. This was not only for defence, it was also to provide shade in the terrible heat of summer.

Most of the typical Azerbaijani private houses have survived in Ordubad, which in the middle of the nineteenth century was an important community; quite a few houses still in existence were built at that time. These houses are two-storeyed; their decorative reception rooms or *ayvans* were octagonal, covered with vaulting. Their entrance gates were topped by semi-domes.

Baku in modern times

Sources from the early seventeenth century onwards often stress that the old core of the city of Baku, the palace of the Shirvanshahs, had been severely damaged as the result of hostilities and wars, when the city was depopulated and its most important medieval buildings lay in ruins.

From the middle of the nineteenth century Baku began to develop again at a rapid pace. With an eye to transport and trade, the new city centre was planned along the seashore, and as the new town developed, the old town lost its importance. When large-scale building was undertaken the old historical quarter was by-passed—this, it was decided, was the easiest solution of all, yet nonetheless quite a number of the more interesting buildings came to be demolished. In the latter half of the nineteenth century, when the town had a population of 112,000, blocks of flats in an eclectic style sprang up like mushrooms. As in other big cities of Europe, imitations of a variety of historical styles were popular. What is today the House of Weddings was French Gothic in style, the headquarters of the Philharmonic Orchestra, Neo-Classical and the "Izmail Palace" Venetian Gothic.

In the first period of town development under socialism, constructivism took over; it has left its mark, for instance, on the Intourist Hotel facing the sea, and the Press Centre. At a later period more traditional and national styles came into favour. Ornate oriental buildings made their appearance, including the Government Headquarters, which towers over the city. Some of the elements seem somewhat discordant; yet the monumental effect of the whole is still overpowering. The House of Sciences is built in the same style.

The most interesting buildings of the 1950s are the Children's Theatre designed by Shulgin, and the new observatory and panoramic cinema on the Kirov Boulevard. Around the same time the Kirov memorial was erected on the highest spot of the city. On the site of the former Black and White Towns have arisen extensive industrial districts and new housing estates.

Metalwork

The art of metalwork in Azerbaijan has a long tradition behind it. The earliest examples of metal ornaments date back to the first millennium BC. Belts, buttons, armlets and anklets of the tenth to the eighth centuries BC, often in silver and gold, are solid and heavy. The forms and motifs show a close kinship to Georgian and Armenian art as, for instance, the armlet with a ram's head, which presumably served as a talisman for its wearer.

The coins minted in Azerbaijan were equally famous. Exquisite examples of this craft, dating from the first millennium BC, were brought to light during the excavations at Hodjal and Karabah.

A choice piece known as the Mingechaur belt which depicts two confronting horses dates back to the fifth century BC. Below the horses a decorative band of geometric patterns runs the length of the belt. The horses undoubtedly reflect Sassanian influence but the geometric motifs and the two-horned animals set between them are more local in origin.

Armlets and anklets with snakes' heads of the first century BC as well as the great many pendants of gold and silver came from the jar burials of Mingechaur. The gold and silver pendants in the shape of a crescent and decorated with a star in the middle are typical of the gold and silversmith's art of Azerbaijan.

The collection of gold objects of Mingechaur displayed in the gold hoard of the Historical Museum of Azerbaijan was produced between the first and eighth centuries AD. The pendants, brooches and other objects in this collection show an astonishing resemblance in both form and decoration to jewellery made today.

The major centres of metalwork in the Middle Ages were Gandja, Barda, Shemakha, Tabriz and Nakhichevan.

Moslem ornamentation took over almost completely in the tenth century AD, due, no doubt, to the fact that there was a lively trade between Azerbaijan and the neighbouring regions, and Moslem motifs would be popular with the Moslem inhabitants of those areas. By that time the jewellery and ornaments of Azerbaijan were highly prized and were taken in lieu of money.

Following the Mongol invasions, new designs were introduced into the Azerbaijani metalwork of the thirteenth century. Chinese, Mongolian and other Far and Near Eastern designs made their appearance. In the fourteenth century Chinese motifs were more frequently encountered: stylized clouds floated, water plants meandered and flowers burst into bloom.

In addition to the local museums, the Hermitage of Leningrad, the Oruzheynaya Palata of Moscow and a number of foreign museums possess collections of Azerbaijani metalwork, dating from the sixteenth century. It was no longer goldsmiths and silversmiths exclusively who worked in metal; they were joined by painters, sculptors and miniaturists. A case in point is the beautiful Azerbaijani silver shield in the Oruzheynaya Palata of Moscow. The outside of the shield is decorated with a finely executed hunting scene: the copy of a detail of a famous miniature by the well-known master Sultan Muhamed. The master is said to have participated in the execution of the reliefs.

In the sixteenth and seventeenth centuries Baku became a centre for finely ornamented arms and armour. Silver armour, shields, daggers, sabres and other weapons were produced. The armour in particular was richly decorated with enamelling, precious stones and exquisite engraving and reliefs. Large numbers of goldsmiths and silversmiths settled in Shemakha, Gandja, Tabriz, Ardebil and other towns in the eighteenth and nineteenth centuries. Whole streets were devoted to their craft, and their guilds dominated certain quarters of the towns.

In the eighteenth century two towns in the Khanate of Shemakha—Legich and Basgol—became noted for their gold and silver work. The exquisitely beautiful Turkish sabres, lances, spears and guns made in Legich, and their intricate gold, silver and copper mountings and inlays vie with the best produced anywhere in the world.

As in other Moslem countries, floral motifs were the most popular, adapted, naturally, to local tastes. Roses, irises, narcissi, tulips, lilies and carnations predominate, and birds are found again and again. The metalwork of Azerbaijan came under a wide variety of influences, but in the course of time these were assimilated into the main local tradition and Azerbaijani work has consequently retained its peculiar folk characteristics to this day.

Carpets

Experts and oral tradition have equally supposed that the original home of the carpet must have been somewhere in the Caucasus. Up to most recent times, however, there was little confirmation for this assumption, since only a few pieces dating from the seventeenth century were known from this region; the majority of existing carpets were produced in the eighteenth century. Recently, however, a carpet 2,400 years old was recovered in the area of Pazyryk in the Altai Mountains, and it has been established that it was made in the territory of Azerbaijan. Carpet-making in Azerbaijan has therefore a long past behind it. The fame of these carpets was due to their exceptionally fine qualities, their peculiar colouring and design. The craft of pattern-making, based on the traditions of popular art, was handed down from one generation to the next. Only woollen yarns of an outstanding quality and of a silken lustre were used; the warp was of cotton.

The characteristics of the carpets changed from district to district. Those belonging to the Shirvan group are small, finely knotted and of a minute design. The central field is filled with stylized geometrically decorative designs, occasionally imitating animals. The ground colour of the carpets may be raspberry red, dark or light blue. They are decorated with squares, ovals, rhombuses, and rosettes made up of stars and configurations in the form of a "T", the pattern in different shades of white, red, pink, brown, golden yellow, turquoise and black.

The best known and at the same time most popular carpets of Azerbaijan and the Caucasus are the Kazak carpets. The Kazak carpets are thick, solid and large. They are generally decorated with a highly coloured, bold pattern. The central field of the Kazak carpet, which exerted a great influence on the Armenian rug, is filled with two or three medallions. These medallions, often bordered by double frames, are in turn filled with hook-shaped figures. Outside the large medallions is a dense network of geometric and floral patterns. The ground colour of the central field is usually green, red, blue or white, bordered with two identical bands. The colours most often encountered on Kazak carpets are white, a lively red, blue, light blue, green, yellow and cream.

The Karabag carpets are best known for their great variety of ornament, which reflect Caucasian and, to some extent, Persian influences. The whole surface of the carpet is covered with ornamentation, mainly floral scrolls, and the ground colour is purple-red and turquoise. The borders are made up of a wide and several narrower bands of patterned flowers. In addition to the two ground colours, green, red, blue, yellow, light blue and cream colour are most frequently use in the design.

"Garden" rugs were also produced in Azerbaijan at the end of the seventeenth and during the eighteenth century. These reflected Persian influence. The central fields contained lakes, trees and swans, designed along formal archaic and symbolic lines, recalling the atmosphere of Egyptian wall paintings.

During the last hundred years carpets containing human figures, groups of people and individual portraits have also been commissioned for special occasions. This produced a completely new genre unknown before, and elicited enormous interest, as shown by the numerous gold medals won at international exhibitions by the artists of Azerbaijan.

Bibliography

Ашурбейли, С.: *Топонимика Апшерона в связи с вопросом этногенезиса азербайджанцев.* Баку, 1967

Аксерова, Н. С.: *Архитектурный орнамент Азербайджана.* Баку, 1959

Азербайджан, Советский Союз. Москва, 1971

Бретаницкий, Л.—Датиев, С.—Мамиконов, Л.—Мотис, Д.: *Нуха.* Москва, 1948

Бретаницкий, Л.—Саламзаде, А.: *Кировобад.* Москва, 1960

Бретаницкий, Л.: *Баку.* Москва, 1965

Бретаницкий, Л.: *Зодчество Азербайджана XII—XV вв. и его место в архитектуре Переднего Востока.* Москва, 1966

Бретаницкий, Л.: *Баку.* Москва—Ленинград, 1970

Цеблынин, У. П.: *Краткий очерк истории дворца ширваншахов в Баку.* Баку, 1939

Дадашев, С. А.: *Памятники азербайджанской архитектуры в Баку.* Баку, 1938

Дадашев, С. А.—Усейнов, М. А.: *Ансамбль дворца ширваншахов в Баку.* Москва, 1965

Glück, H.—Diez, E.: *Kunst des Islam.* Propyläen Kunstgeschichte. Berlin, 1925

Халилев, К.: *Азербайджанская ССР.* Москва, 1972

Кадзиева, М.: *Азербайджан.* Баку, 1960

Касимзаде, Э.: *Проблемы развития азербайджанской советской архитектуры на современном этапе.* Баку, 1967

Керимов, Л.: *Азербайджанский ковер.* Баку, 1967

Ковры Азербайджанской ССР. Москва, 1952

Ledács Kiss, A.—Szütsné Brenner, K.: *Ismerjük meg a keleti szőnyegeket.* Budapest, 1963

Левиатов, В.: *Памятники азербайджанской культуры.* "Бакинский дворец ширваншахов." Баку, 1944

Мамиконов, Л.: *Реставрация части стен бакинской Крепости.* Москва, 1958

Нуриева, А. Я.: *Зодчество Апшерона XVII—XIX вв.* Москва, 1964

Памятники истории Азербайджана. Баку, 1956

Расим, Э.: *Ювелирное искусство Азербайджана.* Баку, 1956

Саламзаде, А.—Абаул Вагаб Рахим оглы: *Архитектура Азербайджана XIV—XIX вв.* Баку, 1964

Sarre, F.: *Die Kunst des alten Persien.* Berlin, 1923

Саркисов, Н.: *Архитектурная керамика Азербайджана.* Москва, 1965

Тулиев, А. Б.: *Азербайджанские ковры и их товароведческая характеристика.* Москва, 1954

Усейнов, М. А.: *Памятники азербайджанского зодчества.* Москва, 1951

Усейнов, М. А. и др.: *История архитектуры Азербайджана.* Баку, 1963

Усейнов, М. А.—Бретаницкий, Л.—Саламзаде, А.: *История архитектуры Азербайджана.* Баку, 1963

List of Plates

33, 34, 35, 36

39, 40, 41

45
46

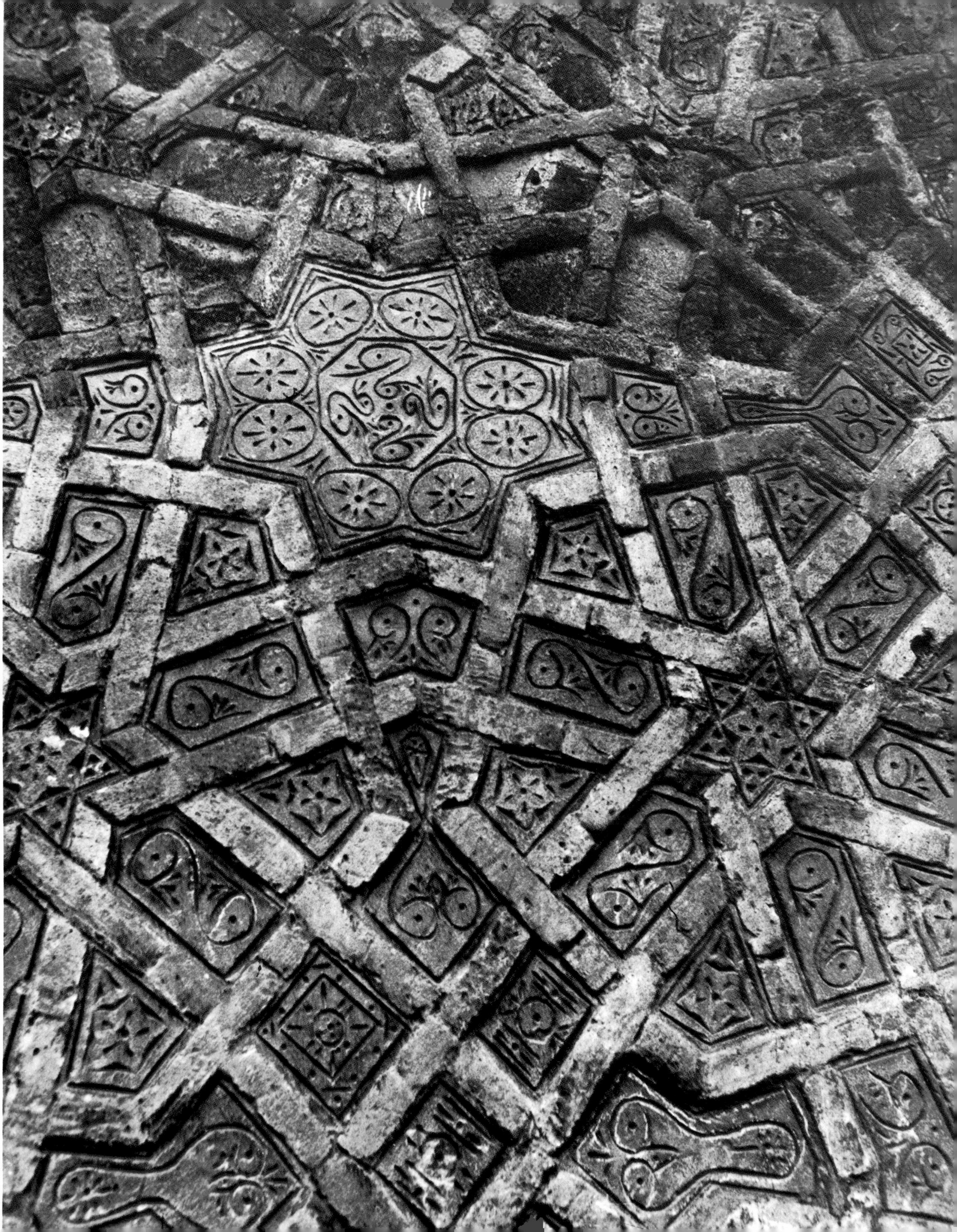

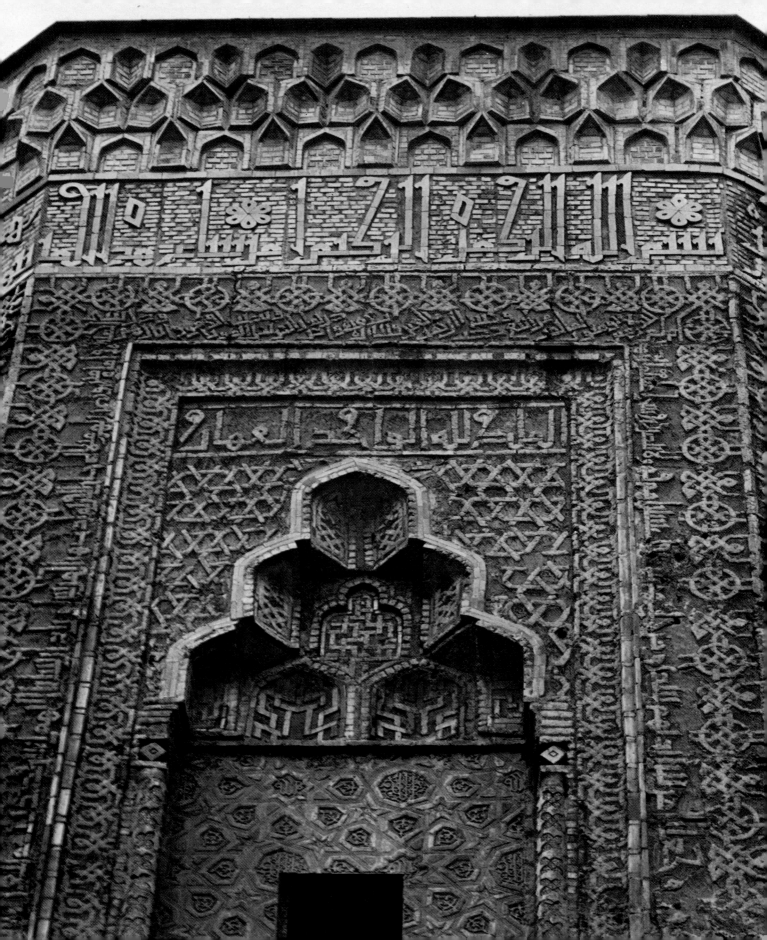

بحضرت مولانا شاه

حرم خاص خانهٔ شاه است

دل عارف که جای الله است

خانهٔ خویش را اصفادارم

76
77

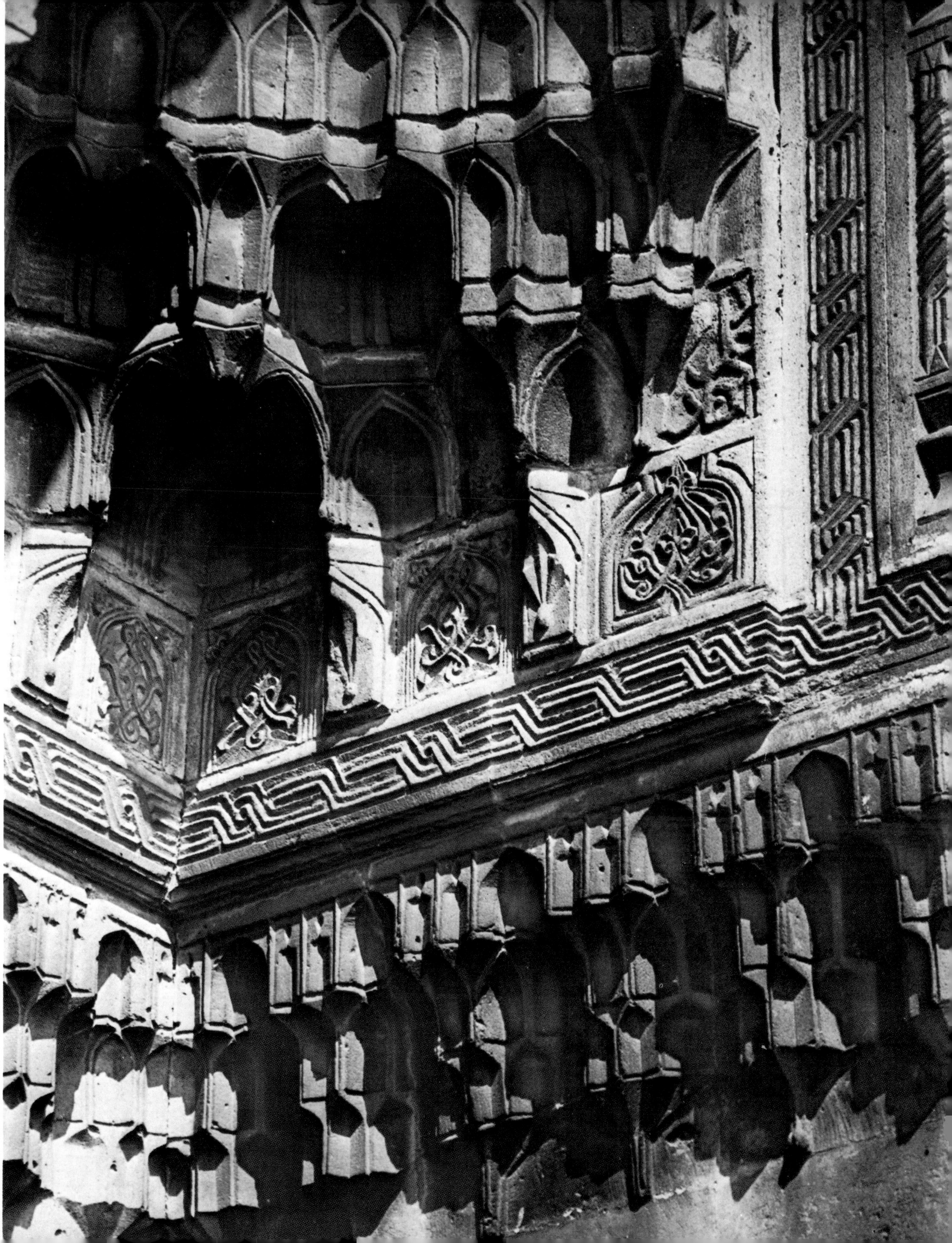

॥ श्री गणेशाय नमः ॥ श्री महाकालिका
जयति श्री विजयराजा तिलका
वत्सर मास हेर रिणाश्र जाल जी
निजि मंदर कणावा महाराज धर्मे
स्वाता दुर्लभित्रि कावली जालेरदाधि
वलाप दशावा जाना भावला किवपतवती
तोप समह बल भेजनो वि अश्र जल
धनल तनि विअ कुलता आम मठी रानक लाल
लिन ना सावला याणि निनो वल्ण वल छनाछ

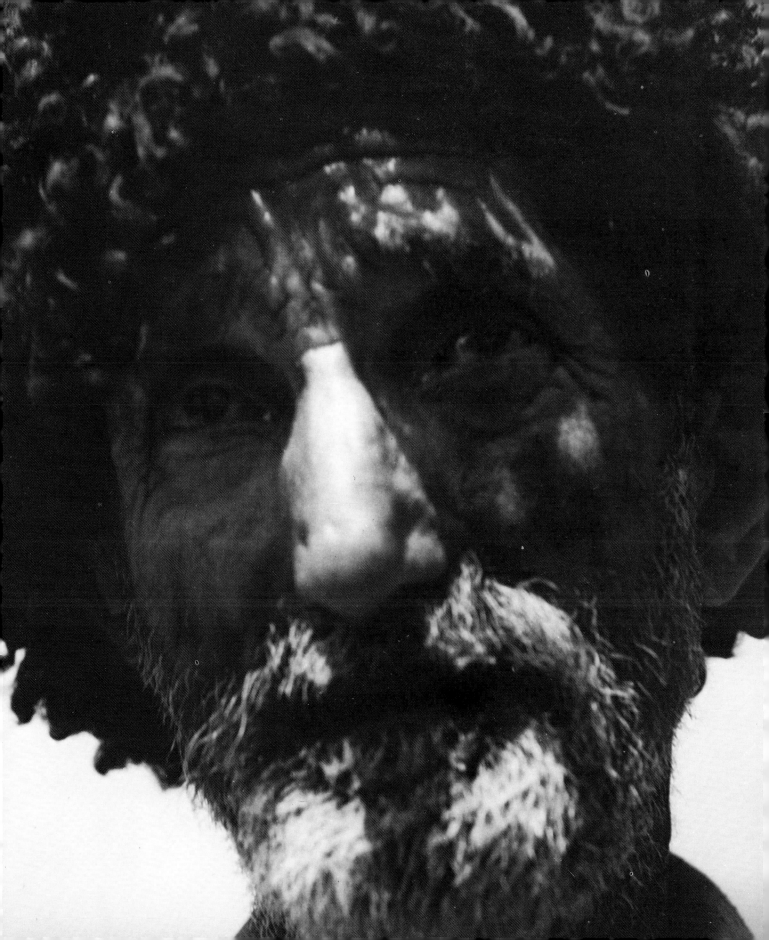

126, 127